JOURNAL FOR THE STUDY OF THE NEW TESTAMENT
SUPPLEMENT SERIES

246

Not the Righteous but Sinners

M.M. Bakhtin's Theory of Aesthetics
and the Problem of Reader–Character
Interaction in Matthew's Gospel

John A. Barnet

T & T CLARK INTERNATIONAL
A Continuum imprint
LONDON • NEW YORK

Copyright © 2003 T&T Clark International
A Continuum imprint

Published by T&T Clark International
The Tower Building, 11 York Road, London SE1 7NX
15 East 26th Street, Suite 1703, New York, NY 10010

www.continuumbooks.com

British Library Cataloguing-in-Publication Data
A catalogue record for this book is available from the British Library

Typeset by ISB Typesetting, Sheffield
Printed on acid-free paper in Great Britain by Bookcraft Ltd, Midsomer Norton, Bath

ISBN 0-8264-6655-9

To

Laura

CONTENTS

ACKNOWLEDGMENTS

This book is a revision of my 2001 doctoral dissertation, which was submitted in the Department of Religion in the Graduate School of Duke University. Many people have contributed to the completion of this project, only some of whom am I able to name here. Truly, my gratitude must be the thanksgiving of John Chrysostom's anaphora, a thanksgiving for all things of which I know and of which I know not, whether manifest or unseen.

First, I would like to thank my teachers, especially the members of my dissertation committee—Moody Smith, Richard Hays and Edna Andrews—without whose encouragement and guidance, both personal and scholarly, this project would never have taken shape. To Fr Paul Tarazi I owe an incalculable debt. He first taught me the sweetness of God's word and to this day continues to remind me of the one thing needful. My deepest gratitude is for my advisor, Dan Via. While his work has provided the foundation for my own first steps, his incisive criticism and compassionate persistence have ensured the completion of this project.

I would also like to thank my students, especially my first students, Bobbie Galuska and Tekla Virvan. Their trustful enthusiasm for the bible classes of a young seminarian many years ago serves as a constant reminder that above all else my task is to feed the people. They too have been my teachers.

I especially would like to thank my parents, Jack and Olga. They have instilled in me the desire for knowledge and understanding. Their example has taught me that knowledge is not yet understanding. Their love and encouragement in the face of my many and varied endeavors have made it possible for me at last to choose the good portion.

Finally, I would like to thank my wife and dialogic partner, Laura. She has been a constant source of support and encouragement throughout this project. Not only has she lived graciously in the shadow of 'that paper', postponing any number of her own projects, but she has also managed to produce a son, Jacob Nicholas, who has joyfully rearranged our lives. Together they have taught me the meaning of gratitude.

ABBREVIATIONS

AB	Anchor Bible
CBQ	*Catholic Biblical Quarterly*
HTR	*Harvard Theological Review*
ICC	International Critical Commentary
Int	*Interpretation*
JR	*Journal of Religion*
JSNT	*Journal for the Study of the New Testament*
JSNTSup	*Journal for the Study of the New Testament*, Supplement Series
NovT	*Novum Testamentum*
NovTSup	*Novum Testamentum*, Supplements
NTS	*New Testament Studies*
TynBul	*Tyndale Bulletin*
TZ	*Theologische Zeitschrift*
VT	*Vetus Testamentum*

Chapter 1

INTRODUCTION

The Problem

When the Pharisees in Matthew's Gospel see Jesus and his disciples at table with tax collectors and sinners, they confront the disciples with their teacher's apparent violation of the rules governing table fellowship. But it is Jesus himself who responds: 'Those who are well have no need of a physician, but those who are sick. Go and learn what this means, "I desire mercy, and not sacrifice". For I came not to call the righteous, but sinners' (9.12-13). The immediate addressees of this scene are, of course, the Pharisees. Also present are the disciples, and presumably, the tax collectors and sinners. Therefore, these words of Jesus could be construed as words intended in some way for each one of these character groups. Ultimately, however, these words are intended for the readers of Matthew's Gospel. But because the readers are not included among the addressees of the narrative world, they must somehow interact with the narrative's character groups in order to be engaged as addressees.

This raises a number of questions. Do the readers participate in the table scene as the omniscient observers of the characters' interaction with one another, or are they encouraged to assume the more limited role of one or more of the characters? When Jesus tells the Pharisees to learn what it means that God desires mercy and not sacrifice, what are the readers expected to do? Are they to understand Jesus' words as a call to hear his words and imitate his behavior? When Jesus says that he calls not the righteous but sinners, how are the readers to understand their own status? Are they the righteous, or are they the sinners? If they are the righteous, is the Gospel still addressed to them? If they are the sinners, how are they to respond?

Scenes of character interaction similar to the table scene are repeated throughout the narrative sections of Matthew's Gospel. The purpose of this study, broadly speaking, is to examine the interaction of the readers of Matthew's Gospel and the narrative's major character groups: the Pharisees, the disciples and the supplicants.

Pharisees, Disciples, Supplicants and Readers

The major character groups of Matthew's Gospel have been defined differently. Janice Capel Anderson, for example, defines five major groups: the Jewish leaders, the disciples, the crowds, the supplicants and the Gentiles.[1] Although Anderson acknowledges that there is some overlap between the supplicants and the Gentiles, she distinguishes the Gentiles 'because of the important role they play in the development of the theme of the justification of mission to the Gentiles'.[2] Jack Dean Kingsbury adopts a similar classification—the disciples, the religious leaders and the crowds—but groups the supplicants and the Gentiles together in a fourth category, which he calls the minor characters.[3] Paul S. Minear, on the other hand, identifies only three major groups: the disciples, the crowds and the Pharisees, who remain throughout the Gospel the core opponents of Jesus.[4] Minear's classification serves his purpose of correlating the character groups in the Gospel's narrative world with historical groups in Matthew's community:

> The twelve disciples correspond to the prophets, wise men, and scribes who were leaders in the churches of the second generation. The crowds of followers match the lay members of these churches. In bitter conflict with both these groups are the Pharisaic leaders of the rival synagogues.[5]

Finally, David R. Bauer identifies only two major groups: the disciples and Israel, which is comprised of the crowds and the religious leaders.[6]

The differences between the various classification schemes suggest that

1. Janice Capel Anderson, 'Matthew: Gender and Reading', *Semeia* 28 (1983), 3-27 (10-11).
2. Anderson, 'Gender and Reading', 11 n. 25.
3. Jack Dean Kingsbury, *Matthew as Story* (Philadelphia: Fortress Press, 2nd edn, 1988), 10.
4. Paul S. Minear, *Matthew: The Teacher's Gospel* (New York: Pilgrim Press, 1982), 10-11. Other scholars have also singled out the Pharisees as the main opponents of Jesus. See, for example, Robert H. Gundry, *Matthew: A Commentary on his Literary and Theological Art* (Grand Rapids, MI: Eerdmans, 1982), 306; and W.D. Davies and Dale C. Allison Jr, *A Critical and Exegetical Commentary on the Gospel According to Saint Matthew* (ICC; 3 vols.; Edinburgh: T. & T. Clark, 1988), I, 302.
5. Minear, *Matthew*, 10-11.
6. David R. Bauer, 'The Major Characters of Matthew's Story: Their Function and Significance', *Int* 46 (1992), 357-67.

character groupings other than the Gospel's most explicit definitions are determined to a considerable extent by the interpreter's perspective. If Anderson distinguishes the Gentiles from the supplicants, it is because she considers Matthew's theme of mission to the Gentiles to be sufficiently important to warrant the distinction. Minear, on the other hand, because he views Matthew's Gospel primarily as a teacher's handbook in the form of a narrative, apparently makes his most basic distinction between those who teach and those who are taught, subsequently fitting his historical correlations into this division.

Essentially, I have adopted Minear's classification of the Pharisees, the disciples and the crowds, emphasizing the role of the supplicants, who would otherwise be part of the crowds. Unlike Minear, however, I do not define the character groupings on the basis of a hypothetical historical reconstruction of Matthew's community; rather, my scheme corresponds to the three types of response that are occasioned by the preaching of the word throughout Matthew's Gospel, which responses are figuratively depicted in the parable of the sower: rejection, unfruitful reception and fruitful comprehension (13.18-23).[7] The Pharisees, indeed the Jewish leadership as a whole, are clearly depicted as those who reject Jesus (12.14) and his teaching (12.2). The disciples, despite their immediate acceptance of Jesus (4.20, 22; 9.9) and the (eventual) comprehension of his teaching (13.51; 16.12), are portrayed as those of little faith (8.26; 14.31; 17.20), who doubt even in the presence of the risen Lord (28.17). In

---

7.   If, as some have argued, ch. 13 constitutes the structural and thematic center of Matthew's Gospel, then the theme of reception as a criterion of character classification is further supported. See, for example, the chiastic outline in C.H. Lohr, 'Oral Techniques in the Gospel of Matthew', *CBQ* 23 (1961), 403-35 (427). See also Peter F. Ellis, *Matthew: His Mind and his Message* (Collegeville, MN: Liturgical Press, 1974), 12-13; and H.J. Bernard Combrink, 'The Structure of the Gospel of Matthew as Narrative', *TynBul* 34 (1983), 61-90. For a summary of the major weaknesses of chiastic approaches to the Gospel, see David R. Bauer, *The Structure of Matthew's Gospel: A Study in Literary Design* (JSNTSup, 31; Sheffield: Almond Press, 1988), 40. These weaknesses, however, do not mitigate the importance of ch. 13 for the Gospel as a whole. See, for example, Dan O. Via Jr, *Self-Deception and Wholeness in Paul and Matthew* (Philadelphia: Fortress Press, 1990), 100. Although Via does not himself propose a chiastic pattern as the overall structure of Matthew's Gospel, he does argue that Mt. 13.1-53 represents the pivotal section of the Gospel's portrayal of the response to Jesus: 'The context on either side develops two different responses to Jesus, while the parabolic discourse in the middle presents the cause for this division and difference.'

other words, they remain until the end of the Gospel unfruitful receivers of the word. It is only the supplicants, in particular the Gentile supplicants, who represent Matthew's fruitful receivers: they alone are commended by Jesus for their great faith (8.10; 15.28), and they alone do not subsequently stumble. Indeed, the very absence of the Gentile supplicants from the subsequent narrative ensures that they remain the narrative's exemplars of great faith. Consequently, when their brief stories are compared to the lengthy narrative of the disciples, which narrative is essentially commensurate with the public ministry of Jesus, an important question is raised: Is fruitful reception possible in the ongoing life of discipleship? Or is it possible only if one somehow repeatedly adopts the posture of the Gentile supplicants, who are portrayed as outsiders and not as members of the character group the disciples?

While this classification of Matthew's characters can be said to correspond to the three types of response that are depicted throughout Matthew's Gospel, it is less clear how this scheme corresponds to the character groupings that are present in the table scene with Jesus. In the first place, the tax collectors and sinners are not themselves portrayed as supplicants: they are simply presented 'at table' with Jesus. Secondly, none of these character groups is depicted in the table scene as responding to the words of Jesus. Nevertheless, it will be argued that the three groups in the table scene not only correspond to the three types of response, but that, more importantly, the interpretation of the table scene is essential for understanding how the readers ultimately are engaged as the addressees of Matthew's Gospel: for if it is correct that Jesus only calls sinners, then it follows that the readers of Matthew's Gospel, who interact with these characters, are themselves addressed as sinners, regardless of their own self-understanding. The interpretation of the table scene, therefore, constitutes one of the main presuppositions of this study.

Jesus Calls Sinners

Jesus sits at table with the tax collectors and sinners (9.10). Presumably he calls them (11.28-30).[8] Certainly, he comes for them (1.22; 26.28). Jesus

---

8.   Gundry, *Matthew*, 168, maintains that Jesus' call is an invitation to the messianic banquet, which the table fellowship anticipates. So also, Heinz J. Held, 'Matthew as Interpreter of the Miracle Stories', in Günther Bornkamm, Gerhard Barth and Heinz J. Held, *Tradition and Interpretation in Matthew* (Philadelphia: Westminster Press, 1963), 165-299 (258). On the other hand, Davies and Allison, *Matthew*, II, 105, are less certain, noting that Matthew leaves unsaid whether Jesus calls sinners to

calls disciples to follow him (4.18-22; 9.9). Does this mean that they are sinners?

It is a commonplace of contemporary gospel criticism to treat the story of Jesus at table with the tax collectors and sinners (9.10-13) as the thematic conclusion of the preceding verse—the call of Matthew (9.9)—despite a change of scene and a shift in interest from Matthew, one particular tax collector, to the tax collectors and sinners in general. Indeed, most scholars do not see the need to explain why these scenes should be read together; they simply accept the division of 9.9-13 as conventional, sometimes even referring to 9.9-13 in its entirety as 'The Call of Levi',[9] more often simply citing it without a title.[10]

Although these scholars implicitly agree that the table scene completes the call of the tax collector Matthew, the fact that Matthew is also one of the Twelve (10.3), a group that is frequently set apart from the crowd for special instruction, does not play a role in their interpretation of the scene.[11] Generally, they conclude that the purpose of the scene is to provide the disciples of Jesus with an example of the merciful behavior that they are expected to follow.[12] And, indeed, there is much to commend in this interpretation: Jesus is clearly portrayed as the central figure of the

repentance, the kingdom or discipleship. Although Davies and Allison are technically correct, an alternative explanation is that these terms represent the various shades that constitute an entire complex of meaning.

9.   E.P. Sanders, *Jesus and Judaism* (Philadelphia: Fortress Press, 1985), 178. Apparently so named because it is considered a triple tradition passage. For the variation 'Jesus Calls Levi', see Davies and Allison, *Matthew*, II, 96.

10.   See Gerhard Barth, 'Matthew's Understanding of the Law', in Günther Bornkamm, Gerhard Barth and Heinz J. Held, *Tradition and Interpretation in Matthew* (Philadelphia: Westminster Press, 1963), 58-164 (82); Gundry, *Matthew*, 165; Held, 'Miracle Stories', 257; Via, *Self-Deception*, 117. The examples could be multiplied. It is interesting to note that a number of these same scholars separate the initial call of the disciples (4.18-22) from the subsequent missionary summary (4.23-25), despite a similar movement from the particular to the general. See, for example, Sanders, *Jesus and Judaism*, 103; Via, *Self-Deception*, 101, 117; David E. Garland, *Reading Matthew: A Literary and Theological Commentary on the First Gospel* (New York: Crossroad, 1993), 48. For the variation 4.18-22 and 4.23-5.2, see Davies and Allison, *Matthew*, I, 392, 410. On the other hand, Gundry, *Matthew*, 61, treats 4.17-25 as an entire unit.

11.   See, for example, Gundry, *Matthew*, 166, who rejects the suggestion that the first evangelist substitutes the name Matthew for Levi to gain a reference to one of the twelve. Gundry cites the evangelist's emphasis on the discipleship of the crowds in this scene, as well as Matthew's obscurity among the twelve.

12.   See Gundry, *Matthew*, 168; Garland, *Reading Matthew*, 104.

table scene, not the tax collectors and sinners, nor the disciple Matthew, who is not mentioned. Furthermore, a plausible explanation for Matthew's use of Hos. 6.6—'I desire mercy and not sacrifice'—is that it is intended to instruct others to perform similar acts of mercy.[13]

Daniel Patte, on the other hand, is one scholar who has noticed a tension when these scenes are read together: in the former scene Jesus demonstrates his authority to deal with the tax collectors and sinners at a distance—by means of his word; in the latter scene he sits at table with them.[14] Nevertheless, Patte argues that the two scenes are indeed directly linked, because 9.13 not only echoes the call of Matthew but explains it: 'When Jesus calls Matthew to discipleship he calls a sinner.'[15] Patte's interpretation—that these scenes form a unified pericope concerning discipleship—suggests an alternative reading: the evangelist does not so much provide an example for others to follow as affirm that those who are with Jesus, including his disciples, are sinners. For if the disciple Matthew is a sinner, and if Jesus does not (apparently) call the righteous, then it follows that all of Jesus' disciples must be sinners. If this interpretation of the table scene is correct, then one should be able to find evidence in Matthew's Gospel that the rest of the disciples are also characterized as sinners.

The earliest call of the disciples (4.18-22) reports nothing of their status; it simply narrates the disciples' immediate obedience to the command of Jesus. The context of the call narrative, on the other hand, records that Jesus begins his ministry in the disciples' home region of Galilee, the

---

13.   Barth, 'Matthew's Understanding of the Law', 83, concludes that 'if Jesus does not shrink from a defiling association with sinners, it is because God himself is gracious and merciful, and therefore desires that we show mercy'. Davies and Allison, *Matthew*, II, 105, fault Barth's interpretation for failing to explain the meaning of 'sacrifice'. Instead, they propose that ελεοσ carries the original connotation of ηεσεδ for Matthew: the Pharisees are criticized, therefore, for lacking the animating spirit of heart-felt covenant loyalty in their Torah observance. Presumably the failure of the Pharisees serves as an invitation for others to fulfill the religious requirement in a spirit of mercy.

14.   Daniel Patte, *The Gospel According to Matthew: A Structural Commentary on Matthew's Faith* (Philadelphia: Fortress Press, 1987), 127-28.

15.   Patte, *Matthew*, 127. So also, Warren Carter, 'Jesus' "I Have Come" Statements in Matthew's Gospel', *CBQ* 60 (1998), 44-62 (54-55). See also Held, 'Miracle Stories', 258, who asserts that Jesus' pronouncement (9.13) unites two originally independent events (9.9; 9.10), thereby serving Matthew's intention of making 'a Christological statement'.

region of darkness and death, the region to which Jesus brings his great light (4.12-16). For Matthew to depict the (prospective) disciples as dwelling in the region of darkness and death is implicitly to characterize them as sinners in need of mercy. This interpretation is confirmed by the repeated citation of Hos. 6.6 (Mt. 9.13; 12.7), which implies that the tax collectors and sinners, on the one hand, and the disciples, on the other, truly are in need of mercy.

Although there is indeed some evidence that the disciples are sinners, such a description, however, does not appear to be the foremost trait of their characterization. In the first place, when the disciples pluck grain on the sabbath (12.1-8), in violation of an apparent Sabbath prohibition, Jesus nevertheless declares them to be guiltless (12.7). Secondly, by questioning the disciples about Jesus' fellowship in the table scene, the Pharisees implicitly acknowledge that they do not consider the disciples to be members of the character group the tax collectors and sinners. This does not mean, however, that the disciples should be considered the righteous. Rather, it suggests that the Gospel's characterization of the disciples is intended to emphasize for the readers a different trait than that of the tax collectors and sinners, both of which traits are necessary if the readers are to be fully engaged by the narrative.

The question then becomes, Is it possible to acknowledge sin as an aspect of the disciples' characterization while at the same time preserving it as the defining trait of the character group the tax collectors and sinners? By analyzing the roles of these character groups with respect to the groups' proximity to the narrative's centers of authority[16]—the Jewish leadership and Jesus—the characterization 'sinner' can indeed be seen in a different light. For if the tax collectors and sinners for whom Jesus comes represent the marginal members of Jewish religious society, then their sin has been defined by the religious elite. On the other hand, if the disciples are portrayed primarily as those who are with Jesus (18.20; 28.20), then their sin is defined instead by Jesus (15.17-20; 18.5-9), or rather, by the evangelist himself.[17]

---

16. See Amy-Jill Levine, *The Social and Ethnic Dimensions of Matthean Salvation History: 'Go Nowhere among the Gentiles...' (Matt. 10.5b)* (Lewiston, NY: Edwin Mellen Press, 1988), 4-8, who analyzes the Gospel's social axis in terms of the categories of center and periphery, which approach is dependent on textual strategies employed by deconstruction and feminist analysis.

17. One of the implications of defining the characters in terms of their proximity to the narrative's centers of authority is that it then becomes possible to classify the

This interpretation poses a special challenge for the readers of Matthew's Gospel, who must interact with each of the narrative's character groups: Jesus does indeed call sinners; the readers, however, are expected to be sensitive to the narrative's various perspectives regarding the definition of 'sinner'.

Jesus Does Not Call the Righteous

When Jesus defends his association with the tax collectors and sinners in the table scene, he not only insists that his purpose is to call the sinners, at the same time he appears to exclude the righteous from his mission: 'For I did not come to call the righteous but sinners' (9.13). W.D. Davies and Dale C. Allison have proposed four interpretations of 9.13 with respect to the status of the righteous.[18] First, the righteous are presumed to be saved; therefore they are not called. Second, the righteous are too stubborn to heed Jesus' call; therefore, again, they are not called. Third, nothing is said about the righteous, one way or the other, as it is the status of the sinners that is emphasized here. Fourth, everyone is assumed to be a sinner, including the righteous; therefore everyone in fact is called. With regard to Matthew's intention, Davies and Allison reject the first interpretation, but see no way of deciding between the remaining possibilities.

Although it is impossible to be certain which of these interpretations best conveys the evangelist's intention, there are indeed compelling reasons to reject the argument that the righteous of 9.13 are excluded because they are presumed to be saved. In the first place, there are several passages in Matthew's Gospel that imply a general sinfulness of humanity: as Davies and Allison note, when Jesus teaches on the mountain, he addresses the crowds (5.1; 7.28), and presumably the disciples (5.1), as evil ones who know how to give good gifts (7.11).[19] Later, when the rich young man asks Jesus the way to life, he is told, 'One there is who is good' (19.17), again an implicit acknowledgment of humanity's sinfulness.[20] Moreover, if, as Davies and Allison contend, the parallel verse, 9.12, transparently equates the strong with those who oppose Jesus,[21] then it is virtually certain that the righteous of 9.13 should also be equated with

---

supplicants together with the tax collectors and sinners, despite the apparent differences of their respective characterizations.

18.   Davies and Allison, *Matthew*, II, 106-107.
19.   Davies and Allison, *Matthew*, II, 107.
20.   Davies and Allison, *Matthew*, III, 43.
21.   Davies and Allison, *Matthew*, II, 103.

the opponents of Jesus. And since the opponents of Jesus in the table scene are the Pharisees, this implies that Jesus is indirectly characterizing them as the strong and the righteous. In view of the sayings of judgment that are elsewhere directed against the Pharisees, such as the Baptist's warning (3.7-12), the parable of the vineyard (21.33-46), and Jesus' woes (23.13-36), it is clear that the Pharisees are not presumed to be saved. And if the Pharisees are not presumed to be saved, then neither are the righteous of 9.13.

Does Jesus exclude the righteous because they are too stubborn to heed his call? Davies and Allison apparently consider 'stubbornness' to be the human refusal to understand, citing in support of this interpretation Jesus' explanation for his parabolic speech (13.14-15).[22] Parables without their interpretive key function in Matthew's Gospel as the sign of failed understanding (13.13), which is clearly the condition of the Pharisees: when Jesus directs them to learn the meaning of Hos. 6.6, it is implied, as David E. Garland concludes, 'that they have failed to understand the basic tenor of the Scripture'.[23] The Pharisees' failure to understand the Scripture is subsequently confirmed when they confront Jesus and his disciples in the grainfields (12.1-8), only to be told that had they understood the meaning of Hos. 6.6 they 'would not have condemned the guiltless' (12.7). Thus it is conceivable that Jesus does not call the righteous—here the Pharisees—because 'he knew it would do no good'.[24]

There are several problems with this interpretation as it stands, however. In the first place, as Dan O. Via has observed, the refusal to understand is also the consequence of divine initiative, whether God withholds the interpretive key of the parables or hardens the heart.[25] Paradoxically, however, divine initiative does not mitigate human responsibility: in the interpretation of the parable of the sower, those who hear the word but do not understand are grouped with those who hear the word but fail to persevere (13.18-22). In other words, everyone who hears the word is responsible to produce the proper fruit. Secondly, and perhaps more importantly, this interpretation fails to explain why, if the Pharisees are too stubborn to heed his call, Jesus would be addressing them at all. Although it is true that Jesus is never portrayed as actually calling the Pharisees, he does address them, sometimes directly (9.12-13; 12.3-8, 11-12, 25-37; 15.3-9;

22. Davies and Allison, *Matthew*, II, 106.
23. Garland, *Reading Matthew*, 104.
24. Davies and Allison, *Matthew*, II, 106.
25. Via, *Self-Deception*, 102.

19.4-9; 22.41-45; 23.13-36), sometimes indirectly in parables (21.28-44; 22.1-14). Nor, finally, does this interpretation explain why the opponents of Jesus should be called 'the righteous'.

Lastly, it has been proposed that the saying 'I did not come to call the righteous but sinners' is ironic: everyone is assumed to be a sinner; therefore everyone is called. The righteous are simply 'those who failed to see that they were no better off than everyone else'.[26] In many respects this is the most compelling of the explanations proposed by Davies and Allison. It takes into consideration the passages that imply a general sinfulness of humanity, such as 7.11 and 19.17. It provides an explanation for characterizing the opponents of Jesus as 'the righteous'—they only appear to be righteous. Finally, it explains why Jesus would continue to address the Pharisees, despite their apparent refusal to understand: presumably they are being called, but not directly.

In order for the call to be effective, however, the Pharisees would have to realize that despite their apparent status as the righteous, they are in fact no better off than the sinners. Apparently the mission of John the Baptist was intended in part to challenge directly the flawed self-understanding of the Pharisees: 'Bear fruit that befits repentance, and do not presume to say to yourselves, "We have Abraham as our father"; for I tell you, God is able from these stones to raise up children to Abraham' (3.8-9). The Baptist's direct approach, however, did not succeed: 'For John came to you in the way of righteousness, and you did not believe him, but the tax collectors and the harlots believed him; and even when you saw it you did not afterward repent and believe him' (21.32). His failure may be attributed to the human tendency to resist direct confrontation. As the ancient rhetorician Demetrius of Phaleron observed, 'great lords and ladies' do not like to be confronted with their faults. Therefore he advised in his rhetoric that they should be corrected indirectly:

> we shall rather blame some other persons who have acted in the same manner. For example, in addressing the tyrant Dionysius, we shall inveigh against the tyrant Phalaris and the cruelty of Phalaris... The hearer is admonished without feeling himself censured.[27]

---

26. Davies and Allison, *Matthew*, II, 107.

27. Demetrius of Phaleron, *On Style* 5.292. Noted by Robert Houston Smith, 'Matthew's Message for Insiders', *Interpretation 46* (1992), 229-39 (237). Also noted by Garland, *Reading Matthew*, 229. Both Smith and Garland cite Demetrius of Phaleron to support the interpretation that Mt. 23 is directed against Matthew's community.

Although it is impossible to prove that Matthew was familiar with this rhetorical commonplace, Scripture itself attests the example of the prophet Nathan obliquely confronting David concerning his adultery with the wife of Uriah the Hittite, a confrontation that leads to David's repentance (2 Sam. 12.1-14). A similar intention would appear to be behind Jesus' telling of the parable of the vineyard (Mt. 21.33-44). When Jesus asks his listeners what the owner of the vineyard will do to the tenants, they (like David) unknowingly convict themselves: 'He will put those wretches to a miserable death, and let out the vineyard to other tenants who will give him the fruits in their seasons' (21.41). Even though the Pharisees do not come to the realization that their status avails them nothing, they at least recognize that the parable is intended to rebuke them: '...they perceived that he was speaking about them' (21.45).

The response of the Pharisees confirms the principle of oblique correction, supporting the interpretation that Jesus calls everyone, at least indirectly. The failure of the Pharisees to reconsider their status as the righteous, however, suggests that Matthew's depiction of the Pharisees' interaction with Jesus is not so much intended to depict a call but to warn others, in particular the disciples of Jesus, regarding the possibility of stubborn blindness. If this interpretation is correct, one would expect to find evidence that the disciples have understood Jesus' correction of the Pharisees. While there is ample evidence that the disciples understand Jesus' teaching (13.51; 16.12), it is less clear that they understand his correction of the Pharisees. Indeed, it is more likely that they do not. For example, after Jesus tells the Pharisees and scribes that for the sake of their traditions they transgress the commandment of God (15.1-9), a clear example of the blindness that characterizes the Pharisees (15.14), the reaction of the disciples is to ask Jesus if he is aware that his saying offended the Pharisees (15.12), arguably an unexpected reaction if the depiction of the disciples is intended to show understanding on their part.

Does Matthew's Gospel Call Sinners?

The absence of an understanding response on the part of the disciples suggests, on the other hand, that Matthew depicts Jesus' confrontations with the Pharisees not in order to warn other characters regarding the possibility of stubborn blindness but to warn his ultimate addressees, the readers of Matthew's Gospel. For example, the immediate addressees of Mt. 23.13-39 are the scribes and Pharisees; but the purpose of the entire discourse, according to Garland, is to warn the Church that 'they had better not be found false stewards like the scribes and Pharisees; for if God did not spare a defiant Jerusalem and its temple, God will just as surely not spare an unfaithful church'.[28] Garland is correct to identify the readers of Matthew's Gospel as the ultimate addressees of the discourse. Unfortunately, however, he does not pursue the implications of this rhetorical strategy for Matthew's readers: it is my contention that the readers are not simply warned; they are in fact cast as the potential opponents of Jesus.[29]

The mechanism of a reading approach that casts the readers as the potential opponents of Jesus is by no means self-evident. As we shall see, it is unlikely that the readers would willingly identify themselves with the narrative opponents of Jesus. It is more likely that the readers would recognize that they are, at least in part, like the opponents. Having recognized their complicity with the posture of Jesus' opponents, presumably the readers would then be able to move to the posture of the supplicants, the positive characters in Matthew's Gospel. The question then becomes, How does this recognition occur? The answer I propose is that this recognition is the product of a type of reader–character interaction that encourages the readers to identify with each of the major characters—the Pharisees, the disciples, and the supplicants—as they interact with Jesus. The readers' identification with the Pharisees, therefore, constitutes only one aspect of the problem of reader–character interaction, albeit the most important one. It is also the one most at odds with prevailing contemporary theory, which, as we shall see, advocates a type of reader–character interaction intended to encourage the readers to accept the values of the Gospel's positive characters, such as the supplicants, and to reject those of the negative characters, such as the Pharisees. It is my contention, however, that only by means of this strategy of reader–character identification are the readers truly engaged as Matthew's addressees. For just as Jesus only came to call the sinners, so also Matthew's Gospel only calls those who recognize that they are the sinners, who acknowledge their need for the one who comes for the sinners. It is by encouraging the readers to

28. Garland, *Reading Matthew*, 229. See also Via, *Self-Deception*, 92, who argues that Matthew's portrayal of the human condition makes it impossible to know whether acts reveal or conceal the heart, despite the evangelist's apparent claim to the contrary (7.16). Consequently, the warning to beware of false prophets (7.15) is turned against the reader: 'Beware of the false prophet in you.'

29. Although my characterization of the readers' role is striking, one need only compare this formulation with Heb. 6.4-6, where the author claims that apostasy is the functional equivalence of crucifying the Son of God, clearly an historical impossibility.

identify with the opponents of Jesus—or to recognize that they are in fact like the opponents—that the Gospel constitutes the readers as sinners, thereby establishing them as the potential recipients of good news.

The State of the Question

Characterization and response constitute the two poles of reader–character interaction. Characterization is 'the way in which an author brings characters to life in a narrative', whether the author shows the characters interacting with other characters or a reliable narrator tells the readers something about the characters.[30] Response is the readers' encounter with the text, which encounter is determined to a considerable extent by how one defines the role of the readers.

The current debate about characterization centers on whether characters in some sense rise to the level of autonomous beings or merely serve the plot.[31] Seymour Chatman has attempted to synthesize a middle ground between character-focused and plot-focused criticism.[32] He concludes that since character and plot are in fact interdependent, the primacy of one over the other is actually a function of the readers' focus. Readers build characters from textual indicators, such as the narrator's statements, statements of other characters, and so on. A character thus becomes a 'paradigm of traits' inferred from these indicators. To the extent that a character is viewed as a paradigm of traits, the character may give the illusion of personality. To the extent that the readers focus on individual indicators, character is subordinated to plot.

Kingsbury, whose literary-critical analysis of Matthew's Gospel is influenced by Chatman's model of story and discourse, offers a typical survey of the Gospel's individual and group characters, primarily in terms of their character traits: Jesus is described as 'saving', 'authoritative', 'enabling', 'compassionate';[33] the disciples as 'loyal', 'obedient', 'authoritative', but also susceptible to bouts of 'little faith', 'enamored of wealth', 'anxious

30. Kingsbury, *Matthew as Story*, 9.

31. See Fred W. Burnett, 'Characterization and Reader Construction of Characters in the Gospels', *Semeia* 63 (1993), 3-28, for a discussion of contemporary approaches to characterization.

32. Seymour Chatman, *Story and Discourse: Narrative Structure in Fiction and Film* (Ithaca, NY: Cornell University Press, 1980), 107-38.

33. Kingsbury, *Matthew as Story*, 10-13.

about their future', 'desirous of power and position';[34] the Jewish leaders as 'evil', 'hypocritical', 'lawless', 'spiritually blind';[35] and the crowds as 'well disposed' toward Jesus, 'helpless', 'astonished' at his miracles, but 'without faith' in Jesus.[36]

Although in each case these traits have been correctly inferred from the narrative's textual indicators, by no means do the resulting character paradigms do justice to the emplotted characters of Matthew's Gospel. This is not simply because the characters so defined have been extracted from the plot; the individual traits themselves are no longer true to the narrative since they too have been removed from their interpersonal contexts. Ironically, Kingsbury's principal motivation for writing his literary-critical analysis was to attend to the story itself, unlike those who seek 'information about historical, social, or religious realities that existed beyond the boundaries of the story in the "real world" of the first century'.[37]

An alternative view of character is the one proposed by David McCracken, based primarily on the work of Mikhail Bakhtin.[38] McCracken argues that characters should be seen not as individuals but as 'interdividuals', that is, as individuals in relationship with others. Characters do not have a fixed essence, *contra* Aristotle, but exhibit changing roles, formed in response to other characters. They live on a threshold between the assertion of another character and their own response, 'expressed in anticipatory words that contain the voices of previous speakers'.[39] McCracken cites the example of Gideon, who is called 'mighty warrior' by the angel of the Lord (Judg. 6.12) despite the hesitation and fear he exhibits during the encounter.[40] The appellation actually challenges Gideon to assume the role of mighty warrior, which means that it is only partially true as a description. In this story the narrative crisis is resolved. But in other stories, such characters as Luke's Martha (Lk. 10.41-42) are abandoned in the moment of crisis. As McCracken explains, 'Martha's response to Jesus' words is not even capable of interpretation; it does not exist. After Jesus' response but before Martha's, the story shifts scene and characters

---

34. Kingsbury, *Matthew as Story*, 13-17.
35. Kingsbury, *Matthew as Story*, 17-24.
36. Kingsbury, *Matthew as Story*, 24-25.
37. Kingsbury, *Matthew as Story*, 2.
38. See David McCracken, 'Character in the Boundary: Bakhtin's Interdividuality in Biblical Narratives', *Semeia* 63 (1993), 29-42.
39. McCracken, 'Character in the Boundary', 31.
40. McCracken, 'Character in the Boundary', 31.

once again.'[41] In both examples the readers are brought to the threshold of the character's decision; in the latter example the readers are left at the threshold, 'with the crisis dramatically defined but not resolved'.[42]

McCracken's analysis focuses primarily on the problem of characterization. Although characterization and response are by definition interdependent, especially in a project defined as the examination of reader–character interaction, this study will focus on the activity of readers; characterization will be examined mainly as it relates to the matter of response. A survey of recent Matthean scholarship reveals basically two approaches to the problem of defining Matthew's readers. The first approach, which emphasizes description, is the redaction-critical preoccupation with Matthew's historical community. The second approach, which emphasizes response proper, is the literary-critical focus on the role of the hypothetical reader embedded in Matthew's text.

Redaction Criticism and Matthew's Community

Since the 1950s redaction criticism has been the dominant method of criticism in Matthean studies. Among the axioms of redaction criticism is the conviction that the evangelist addresses the needs of his community.[43] He does so, however, not merely as the compiler of traditions, but as the 'oldest exegete' of these traditions.[44] Indeed, the circumstances in the community so shape the presentation of his gospel that it should not be viewed primarily as a source of historical information about Jesus of Nazareth: although Matthew's Gospel ostensibly tells the story of the historical Jesus, its intention, according to a redaction-critical reading, is to present the risen Lord as the one who addresses Matthew's community. Matthew accomplishes this, in the words of the redaction critic Gerhard Barth, by writing 'the situation of the Church into the life of the disciples during the earthly activity of Jesus'.[45] The outcome of Matthew's editorial activity is that his readers are made 'a contemporary of the historical

---

41. McCracken, 'Character in the Boundary', 33.

42. McCracken, 'Character in the Boundary', 33.

43. Graham N. Stanton, *A Gospel for a New People: Studies in Matthew* (Edinburgh: T. & T. Clark, 1992), 45-53.

44. Günther Bornkamm, 'The Stilling of the Storm in Matthew', in Günther Bornkamm, Gerhard Barth and Heinz J. Held, *Tradition and Interpretation in Matthew* (Philadelphia: The Westminster Press, 1963), 52-57 (55).

45. Barth, 'Matthew's Understanding of the Law', 111.

Jesus'.[46] This happens in two ways—directly by means of the Gospel's discourse material and indirectly by means of the character interactions in the narrative sections.

In his concluding commission, as the redaction critic Heinz J. Held explains, 'Jesus points his disciples for their teaching activity between Easter and the end of the world to what his discourses in Matthew's Gospel contain by way of example.'[47] If the disciples are to teach the words of Jesus 'by way of example', then practically speaking his words must be addressed directly to Matthew's community. In this case one would expect to find evidence that the evangelist has shaped the discourse material specifically to meet the needs of his community. Redaction critics have attempted to isolate the evangelist's particular emphasis by analyzing the Gospel against its probable sources. Gerhard Barth, for example, has observed that Matthew places a general emphasis on the law's 'abiding validity' for the Church.[48] Barth concludes that this reflects Matthew's intention to correct Christian antinomian heretics who were present in his community. Another redaction critic, Robert Gundry, interprets the Gospel's frequent admonitions to practice love and refrain from judging others as an indication that Matthew's community was a mixed body characterized by a growing coldness of love, intramural betrayal, and a desire to weed out the tares before the time of judgment.[49] One can assume, so it is reasoned, that if Jesus warns his disciples not to practice their piety before men, he does so because at least some of the members of Matthew's community were giving alms in order that they might be praised by others. As redaction critics isolate the community's special circumstances, they in effect begin to construct a portrait of Matthew's historical readers.

If the redaction-critical insight is correct, then it is plausible that the members of Matthew's community would have perceived themselves as the intended addressees, in this case, the intended addressees of the discourses of the historical Jesus. As such, they would have occupied a position similar to that of the disciples, who are the principal narrative recipients of Jesus' teaching, often the sole recipients. The perception of

---

46. Barth, 'Matthew's Understanding of the Law', 111.

47. Held, 'Miracle Stories', 268.

48. Barth, 'Matthew's Understanding of the Law', 159-64.

49. Robert H. Gundry, 'A Responsive Evaluation of the Social History of the Matthean Community in Roman Syria', in David L. Balch (ed.), *The Social History of the Matthean Community: Cross-Disciplinary Approaches* (Philadelphia: Fortress Press, 1991), 62-67 (66-67).

role equivalence has led a number of redaction critics to conclude that the character group the disciples is transparent of Matthew's community. This means that the disciples are to be viewed as standing in the place of the members of Matthew's community. In this case, the transparency concept functions as an invitation for Matthew's historical readers to identify with the character group the disciples.

The second way that Matthew's readers are made contemporaries of the historical Jesus is that they are engaged by the Gospel's narrative material, again by means of the transparency concept. For example, according to Held's analysis, the Matthean miracle stories have been 'cut to fit the situation of the Church'.[50] One of the distinctive characteristics of Matthew's Gospel is that only the disciples and the supplicants address Jesus as 'Lord', which most commentators interpret as a sign of divine majesty reflecting the post-resurrection understanding of the Church. Once again, the disciples are said to be transparent of Matthew's community.

Since the disciples in Matthew's Gospel are portrayed ambiguously, however, the transparency concept, which is said to encourage Matthew's historical readers to identify with the disciples, presents the readers with a paradoxical kind of identification. On the one hand, the disciples are the special recipients of Jesus' teaching, possessed of the type of initial understanding that leads to more understanding (13.11-12). On the other hand, they are also characterized as having little faith and a deficient form of understanding, which Held interprets as a type of non-understanding: when the disciples ask Jesus for an explanation of the parable of the weeds, they 'at the same time designate themselves indirectly as lacking in understanding'.[51] The fact that the disciples reach understanding after instruction by Jesus (13.51; 16.12; 17.13) leads Held to conclude that the explanation for their deficient understanding is not to be found in Matthew's supposedly careless editing of his Markan source but in the situation of Matthew's community: Matthew's historical readers themselves are characterized by a type of non-understanding, namely, the deficient understanding of those who confess Jesus as the risen Lord but do not fully understand his teaching.[52] In other words, the transparency

---

50. Held, 'Miracle Stories', 268.
51. Held, 'Miracle Stories', 292.
52. Held, 'Miracle Stories', 292. Although Held does not explain the nature of a believer's non-understanding, by linking it to his subsequent discussion of 'little faith', which he interprets to be an expression of a believer's anxiety (292-96), he implies a

concept should not be seen here as an invitation to identify with the disciples, if identification is understood as emulation of their behavior. Rather, the disciples are transparent of Matthew's community inasmuch as both the disciples and the members of the evangelist's community possess a deficient form of understanding, which Matthew's historical readers are expected to recognize.

Held proposes a similar interpretation for the failure on the part of the disciples to manifest adequate faith. As is well known, faith in Matthew's Gospel is closely connected with miracle, with faith providing the basis for miracle.[53] The disciples, however, who are granted authority to perform miracles (10.1), 'are never shown in Matthew's Gospel in victorious possession of [this] miraculous power'.[54] Rather, they are characterized by doubt and little faith, as on the occasion when they are unable to heal the epileptic boy (17.20). Their failure becomes the opportunity for Jesus to instruct the disciples on the true nature of faith, which *is* manifested by those who are not disciples, namely, the supplicants. Held believes that the evangelist intends by this mixed portrayal of faith once again to address the needs of his community: Matthew's readers themselves are characterized by little faith, which is 'a situation of unbelief within the life of believers'.[55] In other words, 'little faith' is Matthew's designation for those who confess Jesus as the risen Lord, but who are unable to handle the pressure of 'the facts of this world' and therefore live a failed form of discipleship.[56] Consequently, Matthew's community is in need of 'instruction on the nature and the promise of suppliant faith'.[57] On the one hand, Matthew's instruction is intended to assure his community that the Lord will respond to praying faith, just as he responded to the exemplary faith of the supplicants.[58] But Matthew's instruction also warns his community that a broken form of faith, which is not yet unbelief, is not only possible within the community of believers, it in fact describes their condition.

One of the presuppositions of the redaction critics' community descriptions, or reconstructions, is that the text provides a reliable indication of

distinction between conceptual and existential understanding, which is made by Via, *Self-Deception*, 111.

53.   See Held, 'Miracle Stories', 275-96.
54.   Held, 'Miracle Stories', 291.
55.   Held, 'Miracle Stories', 294.
56.   Held, 'Miracle Stories', 296.
57.   Held, 'Miracle Stories', 297.
58.   Held, 'Miracle Stories', 288.

what was actually happening in Matthew's community. Yet without additional information it is impossible to say whether these reconstructions accurately portray Matthew's historical audience. Recently, Graham N. Stanton, who considers the possibility of discerning the readers' circumstances from the text to be axiomatic, has cautioned against assuming that the evangelist's perspective 'is *directly* related to the views and circumstances of the addressees'.[59] When the evangelist admonishes his readers, he may very well be attacking a specific group. On the other hand, it is also possible that 'the evangelist may have in mind several different groups, or he may be addressing his readers in very general terms'.[60]

In his study of the Matthean miracle stories Held does not make Matthew's community the explicit focus of his analysis. Rather, he examines these stories for the purpose of determining the evangelist's theology, especially with respect to the major themes of discipleship and faith. Nevertheless, Held does also characterize Matthew's community, which, according to redaction-critical presuppositions, can be inferred from the Gospel. Held's description of Matthew's community, however, tends to be of a general sort, reflecting his primary interest in the evangelist's theology. Likewise, when Günther Bornkamm interprets Matthew's story of the stilling of the storm (8.23-27) as 'a description of the dangers against which Jesus warns *anyone* who over-thoughtlessly presses to become a disciple',[61] he deepens the readers' understanding of Matthew's teaching on discipleship, not their knowledge of Matthew's historical audience.

While redaction critics are by definition optimistic about the possibility of reconstructing Matthew's community, literary critics are usually not. Dan Via, for example, contends that gospel critics simply lack the 'clear and definite evidence from that real world' that is necessary to 'determine the degree to which a Gospel's narrative world approximates the real world in which the Gospel was written'.[62] The inability of redaction critics to achieve greater certainty in their community reconstructions is, however, not necessarily fatal to their project: for the most part redaction critics have focused their attention on the evangelist's theology, considering the Gospel's possible social situation only insofar as it may help them to clarify the author's intention. This probably explains the tendency of redaction

---

59. Stanton, *Gospel*, 45 (emphasis in original).
60. Stanton, *Gospel*, 48.
61. Bornkamm, 'Stilling of the Storm', 57 (emphasis added).
62. Dan O. Via, Jr, *The Revelation of God and/as Human Reception in the New Testament* (Harrisburg, PA: Trinity Press International, 1997), 101.

critics to imply a generalized, hypothetical reader in place of the concrete, historically situated readers of Matthew's original audience. Indeed, any reconstruction of Matthew's community, especially one that relies primarily on his text, is by definition hypothetical, since we do not have any documentary evidence of Matthew's actual historical readers.

This does not mean, however, that the reconstructions of redaction critics are of no use. What emerges from their work is the portrait of a hypothetical audience, which the Gospel itself implies, rather than the description of Matthew's actual historical audience. Whether or not the portrayed audience represents an accurate description of Matthew's actual historical audience is in fact irrelevant for the purposes of this study. Even if we were able to discover sufficient real-world evidence to reconstruct Matthew's community with great certainty, we would still be unable to say how the actual readers of Matthew's community responded to his Gospel.

Literary Criticism and the Implied Reader
In recent years Matthean scholars have increasingly turned to literary-critical methods, namely, narrative criticism and reader-response criticism. Unlike redaction critics, whose observations about reader reception have been for the most part 'fortuitous',[63] literary critics have made the reader the explicit object of their study. Although there are certainly differences between narrative criticism and reader-response criticism, as practiced by gospel critics the differences have been primarily ones of emphasis. As Stephen D. Moore explains, narrative critics analyze the features of gospel narrative, such as plot, character, point of view, narrative time, even the intratextual reader. Reader-response critics, on the other hand, focus on the 'successive experience of an intratextual reader', which is determined by the other gospel features, namely, plot, character, point of view and narrative time.[64]

Matthean scholars who use literary-critical methods often adopt a version of Wolfgang Iser's intratextual reader called the 'implied reader'.[65] Kingsbury's explanation of the implied reader is representative of New Testament literary critics:

63. Robert M. Fowler, *Loaves and Fishes: The Function of the Feeding Stories in the Gospel of Mark* (Chico, CA: Scholars Press, 1981), 149.

64. Stephen D. Moore, *Literary Criticism and the Gospels: The Theoretical Challenge* (New Haven: Yale University Press, 1989), 180, 183.

65. Wolfgang Iser, *The Act of Reading: A Theory of Aesthetic Response* (Baltimore: The Johns Hopkins University Press, 1978), 34-38.

the term 'implied reader' denotes no flesh-and-blood person of any century. Instead, it refers to an imaginary person who is to be envisaged, in perusing Matthew's story, as responding to the text at every point with whatever emotion, understanding, or knowledge the text ideally calls for.[66]

As this explanation indicates, there are several ways that the implied reader is distinguished from actual readers. One is that the implied reader lacks any social location, except what might be imposed by the text, usually in the form of presupposed historical or social knowledge. Another, as Janice Anderson explains, is that the implied reader is not an actual reader but a construct that 'includes the textual structure which must be realized as well as the structured act of realization'.[67] This usually means that the implied reader is to be understood as the accumulation of the text's intended effects. The role of actual readers in the production of meaning is fulfilled primarily 'by supplying the portions in the narrative which are not written but implied'.[68]

One implication of defining actual reader participation primarily as the filling of textual gaps is that it tends to extend the range of a text's possible meanings. The pervasiveness of competing interpretations on the part of professional readers is strong evidence that readers fill textual gaps differently. For this reason, as Moore contends, reader-oriented gospel critics for the most part have relegated the 'individualistic, actual reader-side of [Iser's model] to the margins'.[69] Consequently, they continue to operate within their customary author-oriented context, despite often using the terminology of reader-response criticism. David B. Howell is typical of gospel critics when he writes that 'the biblical literary critic who adopts some of the critical assumptions of reader-response criticism must take care not to focus too much attention on the act of reception by the reader'.[70] Howell's intention is to limit the range of the possible meanings of a text. Therefore, when he constructs the responses of a hypothetical reader, he focuses on the textually structured aspect of Iser's model. By analyzing the responses of a hypothetical reader, the literary critic, in Howell's words, 'can identify some of the possible effects the Gospel narrative

---

66. Kingsbury, *Matthew as Story*, 38. See also, Richard A. Edwards, *Matthew's Story of Jesus* (Philadelphia: Fortress Press, 1985), 10.

67. Anderson, 'Gender and Reading', 8 n. 19.

68. David B. Howell, *Matthew's Inclusive Story: A Study in the Narrative Rhetoric of the First Gospel* (JSNTSup, 31; Sheffield: JSOT Press, 1990), 38.

69. Moore, *Literary Criticism and the Gospels*, 102.

70. Howell, *Matthew's Inclusive Story*, 41.

might have on an actual reader—effects and meanings which the evangelist may have been trying to achieve in writing the Gospel'.[71] To argue, as Howell does, however, that the proper activity of the gospel critic is to identify the intended effects and meanings of the evangelist is to privilege an author-oriented interpretation of the text, even though he somewhat softens his assertion by speaking of 'possible effects'.

When gospel critics describe the interaction between reader and text using the implied reader construct, they usually emphasize the sequential-temporal dimension of reading, which is essentially, as Howell explains, a process of anticipation and retrospection: 'Hypotheses about what will happen are formed, confirmed, or altered in the time flow of reading as new information and events become available.'[72] Although reader-response critics occasionally make note of the affective side of the sequential-temporal dimension of reading, more often they analyze the way that it communicates information and encourages acceptance of the author's values.

According to the sequential-temporal paradigm, special significance is attached to information that is provided at the beginning of the narrative. This information creates initial reader expectations, which guide the reader's apprehension of all subsequent material. For example, Matthew's Gospel begins with the positive characterization of Jesus, who is presented as the fulfillment of God's plan (1.1-17, 22-23; 2.13, 23; 3.17). This information is not available to the characters in the story;[73] only the implied reader is given this 'frame of reference for interpreting subsequent events'.[74] In other words, the implied reader understands that the words and deeds of Jesus should be authoritative for the characters in the story. Consequently, the implied reader is able to evaluate the characters in terms of their response to Jesus: when the characters respond positively, the implied reader judges them favorably. A favorable evaluation, in turn, creates sympathy for the characters and encourages the implied reader to identify with them.[75] The influence of initial information in determining

---

71. Howell, *Matthew's Inclusive Story*, 42.

72. Howell, *Matthew's Inclusive Story*, 243.

73. Arguably the Father's statement in 3.17, which the evangelist transforms from a personal address (in Mark) into a declaration, is intended only for Matthew's readers. So Gundry, *Matthew*, 52-53; Garland, *Reading Matthew*, 37. On the other hand, Davies and Allison, *Matthew*, I, 339, contend that Matthew's redaction 'makes the event more public', implying that the statement is available to the characters.

74. Howell, *Matthew's Inclusive Story*, 245.

75. Howell, *Matthew's Inclusive Story*, 246.

reader expectation is considerably enhanced when reader-response critics adopt the literary construct of a first-time reader.[76] This is because the first-time reader, by definition, reads the narrative 'with an open mind'.[77]

Identification between the implied reader and the characters who are portrayed in a positive manner is an important means of encouraging actual readers to accept the author's value system, which in Matthew's Gospel coincides with the words and deeds of Jesus. For example, the initial characterization of the disciples is positive, because they respond positively to Jesus' call (4.18-22). Therefore, the implied reader is encouraged to identify with the disciples, especially in their subsequent role as the recipients of Jesus' teaching (5.1; 10.1; 13.10; 13.36; 18.1; 24.3). In this way, the disciples 'become the link whereby the readers become connected to the teaching of the earthly Jesus'.[78] On the other hand, the disciples are also portrayed negatively. Therefore, the implied reader is expected to discern the difference between the behavior of the disciples, which often falls short of Jesus' expectations, and the function of the disciples, which is to serve as the recipients of his teaching. In other words, the implied reader is called to emulate the function of the disciples, but not their behavior. Actual readers are challenged by the disciples' ambiguous portrayal 'to assume the role of the implied reader, and in doing so, to be fully obedient to Jesus in ways in which the disciples have failed'.[79]

Matthew's positive portrayal of the supplicants as those who manifest paradigmatic faith also encourages reader identification, even though the supplicants do not subsequently become members of the character group the disciples.[80] The evaluation of the supplicants with respect to the matter of discipleship depends, as Anderson has observed, 'on whether "discipleship" is viewed as membership in the character group "the disciples" or as the proper response to [sic] belief in Jesus'.[81] In one sense, the evaluation of the supplicants with respect to the matter of discipleship is unimportant: it is the positive response of the supplicants, not their group membership,

---

76. See, for example, Edwards, *Matthew's Story*, 9.

77. Howell, *Matthew's Inclusive Story*, 244.

78. Howell, *Matthew's Inclusive Story*, 246.

79. Howell, *Matthew's Inclusive Story*, 247.

80. Jesus gives authority to the twelve over unclean spirits (10.1), eats the Passover with the twelve (26.20), and commissions the eleven to make disciples of all the nations (28.16-20).

81. Anderson, 'Gender and Reading', 16.

that invites the implied reader to identify with them, just as the implied reader initially identifies with the disciples. Unlike the disciples, however, these minor characters do not subsequently stumble. Consequently, their response to Jesus is instructive for the implied reader: it embodies an aspect of discipleship that the disciples themselves are unable to manifest. Ultimately, therefore, the status of the supplicants as outsiders is significant, as significant as their exemplary faith. Otherwise, as Anderson suggests, 'the supplicants' function as foils would be limited if they became disciples'.[82] The negative characterization of the Jewish leaders, on the other hand, encourages the implied reader to repudiate them and their value system. Although the implied reader does not identify with the Jewish leaders, nevertheless, 'their rejection of Jesus is instructive insofar as their opposition provides the implied reader with a negative example'.[83]

Presumably these examples of positive and negative characterization are also available to the disciples, who are present when the other characters interact with Jesus. According to this type of reading approach, however, the disciples should not be seen as 'the means whereby the readers of Matthew's community come to be included in the plotted story of the earthly Jesus'.[84] Such an interpretation virtually identifies the implied reader, and therefore all actual readers, with the disciples in Matthew's Gospel. What is not available to the disciples, however, is the narrator's commentary, a reminder that the ultimate addressees of these character interactions are the readers of Matthew's Gospel, not the character group the disciples. Therefore, as Howell insists, '[a]ll character groups in the Gospel...contribute to the portrait of the implied reader, but none should be identified with this portrait. The implied reader is superior to every character who interacts with Jesus'.[85] From this vantage point, the implied reader evaluates the responses of the various character groups, identifying with the positive characters and judging the negative ones, in the process actualizing the implied author's value system. Actual readers, according to Howell, are challenged to assume the role of the implied reader, judging and correcting themselves in terms of the implied reader's actualization of the textual structure.[86]

82. Anderson, 'Gender and Reading', 17.

83. Howell, *Matthew's Inclusive Story*, 237.

84. Howell, *Matthew's Inclusive Story*, 229.

85. Howell, *Matthew's Inclusive Story*, 242.

86. Howell, *Matthew's Inclusive Story*, 247. So also Anderson, 'Gender and Reading', 24: 'A single reader might see his or her own worldview partially embodied

Notwithstanding the recent popularity of the implied reader construct in Matthean studies, critics have identified some problems with the theory. The most important criticism concerns the concept's bi-functional definition of textual structure and structured act. The intention of the composite definition is to free the implied reader from being a wholly text-immanent construct, by including the activity of real readers as an essential component of the production of meaning. One of the implications of including a role for real readers is that they bring their historical-cultural background to the process of reading, which Iser considers necessary for actualizing the text. Responding to Wayne Booth's axiom that the most successful reading is the one in which the reader subordinates '[the reader's] mind and heart to the book',[87] Iser asserts the opposite:

> The sacrifice of the real reader's own beliefs, would mean the loss of the whole repertoire of historical norms and values, and this in turn would entail the loss of the tension which is a precondition for the processing and for the comprehension that follows it.[88]

Furthermore, when real readers bring their unique historical values and experiences to the text, they are likely to fulfill the implied reader's role differently. The resulting polyvalence is not only possible but appropriate, according to Iser, inasmuch as each actualization 'represents a selective realization of the implied reader', rather than an exhaustive one.[89]

While it is undoubted that Iser's concept calls for the participation of real readers in order to transform a text into a work, the implied reader construct itself appears to favor the textual structure side of the bi-functional definition: the implied reader is a reader of no particular historical situation; indeed, the implied reader is not really even a reader, but, in Iser's words, 'a network of response-inviting structures', 'a particular role to play', 'a construct and in no way to be identified with any real reader'.[90] These descriptions of the implied reader construct sound very much like Iser's definition of the hypothetical contemporary reader: when the contemporary reader is reconstructed from the text itself, rather than from

in the Jewish leaders, the crowds, the disciples, or any combination of character groups. If an actual reader assumes the role of the implied reader, he or she will evaluate all ideological points of view from the aligned perspectives of the narrator and Jesus.'

87. Wayne C. Booth, *The Rhetoric of Fiction* (Chicago: University of Chicago Press, 1961), 138.

88. Iser, *The Act of Reading*, 37.

89. Iser, *The Act of Reading*, 37.

90. Iser, *The Act of Reading*, 34.

extant documentary evidence of reader reception, it 'represents the role which the author intended the reader to assume'.[91] If Iser can speak of an 'intended role', or elsewhere of 'the ultimate meaning of the text',[92] then it appears, as David Shepherd argues, that the textual structure has been allowed to reassert 'its traditional dominance'.[93] Indeed, Iser himself seems to acknowledge the text's dominance, even while affirming the contribution of real readers: 'Generally, the role prescribed by the text will be the stronger, but the reader's own disposition will never disappear totally; it will tend instead to form the background to and a frame of reference for the act of grasping.'[94] It is precisely this movement 'to and fro from text to reader', suggests Robert Holub, that has allowed Iser's detractors to see 'a deficiency in rigor' where his supporters see 'an abundance of sophistication'.[95]

Another criticism of the implied reader, at least as the construct has been appropriated by some gospel critics, is directed against its emphasis on the sequential-temporal dimension of reading. Actual readers do not seem to experience the reading process in the same way that the implied reader does: Stephen Moore's inability to find evidence that actual readers are 'frustrated, thwarted, discomfited, startled, challenged, puzzled, or enlightened' prompts him to question whether even the gospel critic is manipulated by the text in this manner.[96] A possible explanation for the disjunction between the experience of actual readers and the theoretical responses of the implied reader is that the construct presupposes, if not exactly a first-time reader, then at least one who is constrained by the limitations imposed by the sequential-temporal experience of reading, whereas the evidence concerning the historical reception of Matthew's Gospel suggests that actual readers were (and are) already familiar with the story:

91.   Iser, *The Act of Reading*, 28. On the other hand, if the contemporary reader is reconstructed from documented reactions, then the contemporary reader is said to be real.

92.   Iser, *The Act of Reading*, 98.

93.   David Shepherd, 'The Authority of Meanings and the Meanings of Authority: Some Problems in the Theory of Reading', *Poetics Today* 7.1 (1986), 129-45 (133).

94.   Iser, *The Act of Reading*, 37.

95.   Robert C. Holub, *Reception Theory: A Critical Introduction* (London: Methuen, 1984), 85.

96.   Moore, *Literary Criticism and the Gospels*, 106. The model's allowance for polyvalence implies, of course, that other readers might well have the very experience of reading that has escaped Stephen Moore.

> Christians (or non-Christians for that matter) are unlikely to have become acquainted with Matthew by means of an oral performance of the whole gospel. They are much more likely to have heard shorter sections. They may well have been acquainted with Mark's gospel before Matthew's. In other words, for most of the first recipients, Matthew's gospel was an extended commentary on what the original readers and listeners already knew. Hence the story-line and the plot contained few surprises.[97]

Whether this is true of all readers, it is certainly the case with gospel critics. This suggests that gospel critics who use the implied reader construct do not so much describe what happens during the reading process as define the moves of their ideal reader, moves that have been rehearsed during successive encounters with the text.

Scholarly Consensus
When gospel critics study the interaction of the reader and Matthew's characters, they tend to reach similar conclusions, despite using different methodologies. Although it is anachronistic to speak of redaction critics in terms of the reader-response paradigm, redaction critics often make comments concerning the intended responses of Matthew's original audience. The redaction critics surveyed above consider the disciples to be paradigmatic for Matthew's readers, inasmuch as they are the recipients of Jesus' teaching. The failure of the disciples to manifest adequate faith, which redaction critics often interpret as descriptive of the mixed state of Matthew's community, is compared to the exemplary response of the supplicants. Although the supplicants are not disciples, Matthew's readers are encouraged to emulate their great faith. The Pharisees, on the other hand, despite standing in the place of the leaders of emerging Rabbinical Judaism, who were opposed to Matthew's community, clarify the demands of discipleship by providing Matthew's readers with examples of teaching and behavior that are rejected by Jesus.

Narrative critics and reader-response critics reach similar conclusions, even though their approaches to the Gospel are (purportedly) text- and reader-oriented rather than author-oriented, as in the case of redaction critics. Those considered above view the disciples to be the connecting link between Jesus (and his teaching) and the readers of Matthew's Gospel. The supplicants and Pharisees serve as foils complementing the true meaning of discipleship: the supplicants as models of great faith and the

97. Stanton, *Gospel*, 76.

Pharisees as examples of hypocrisy. In other words, both the historical critics and the literary critics view the supplicants as positive, exemplary characters, the Pharisees as negative characters whose teaching and behavior are to be avoided, and the disciples as mixed characters whose role as the recipients of Jesus' teaching is exemplary.[98] Despite the apparent agreement of these different approaches, I shall propose an alternative reading.

As some scholars have observed, the supplicants who manifest great faith are also individuals who are marginalized or otherwise in need, such as the centurion and the Canaanite woman.[99] This characterization of the supplicants suggests the possibility that great faith may be related to need, in particular, to the recognition of need. If this is correct, what would it mean to say that the supplicants serve as models of faith for the readers to emulate? In other words, if I do not recognize my own need, is it really possible for me to manifest great faith? Similarly, many scholars have observed that the Pharisees are guilty of hypocrisy, which they generally understand as the failure of word and deed to correspond. This definition of hypocrisy has been challenged by Dan Via, who argues that hypocrisy in Matthew's Gospel is actually the non-correspondence of inner disposition and deed, which non-correspondence, despite being intentional, may not be immediately available to one's conscious awareness.[100] Consequently, if awareness of hypocrisy in Matthew's Gospel is not immediately available, what does it mean to say that the Pharisees serve as examples of behavior for the readers to avoid? In other words, if hypocrisy is a form of self-deception, once I am in the condition of self-deception, can I really avoid that which I do not see?

The Proposed Study

The alternative reading that I shall propose is not intended as a refutation of the apparent scholarly consensus. To a great extent interpretive

---

98. An important difference is that historical critics understand the disciples' inadequate faith as descriptive of Matthew's community, whereas literary critics view it as a device to frustrate reader identification, thereby encouraging readers to look to Jesus for exemplary behavior.

99. See Anderson, 'Gender and Reading', 10-17; Levine, *Matthean Salvation History*, 107-64.

100. Via, *Self-Deception*, 17, argues that hypocrisy is a form of self-deception, a paradoxical holding of 'two contradictory beliefs simultaneously'. Although self-deception is intentional, the repressed matter is at the same time inaccessible without some 'special scrutiny or outside help'.

conclusions are dependent upon one's choice of methodology. The fact that gospel critics have reached similar conclusions regarding reader–character interaction, despite using different methodologies, may indicate that they have achieved an assured result. On the other hand, it may simply mean that their methodologies are in fact not appreciably different. The latter may well be the case: as Stephen Moore has concluded, 'reader-response criticism in gospel studies is largely an extension of narrative criticism, and both remain close to author-oriented redaction criticism'.[101]

A Different Model of Communication
One of the common presuppositions of most professional readers of Matthew's Gospel, and a possible explanation for their similar conclusions, has been their reliance upon the same model of communication, which describes a speaker who formulates a message and sends it to a listener who decodes it. Some years ago, the Russian theorist Mikhail Bakhtin, whose body of work spans nearly six decades until his death in 1975, challenged the standard model of communication by radically reconceptualizing the very nature of language as dialogic event. In a piece written during his last years, Bakhtin characterizes the word (and therefore any text) as the confluence of three voices, none of which alone determines meaning:

> The word cannot be assigned to a single speaker. The author (speaker) has his own inalienable right to the word, but the listener also has his rights, and those whose voices are heard in the word before the author comes upon it also have their rights (after all, there are no words that belong to no one). The word is a drama in which three characters participate (it is not a duet, but a trio).[102]

101. Moore, *Literary Criticism and the Gospels*, 73. The tendency among critics to remain close to their familiar methodologies is not limited to those who analyze the gospels. Several years ago Jane P. Tompkins, 'The Reader in History: The Changing Shape of Literary Response', in *idem* (ed.), *Reader-Response Criticism: From Formalism to Post-Structuralism* (Baltimore: The John Hopkins University Press, 1980), 201-32 (224-26), concluded that, despite recent critical attention to the responses of readers, contemporary methodologies have retained an essentially text-immanent or formalist conception of the text.

102. M.M. Bakhtin, 'The Problem of the Text in Linguistics, Philosophy, and the Human Sciences: An Experiment in Philosophical Analysis', in Caryl Emerson and Michael Holquist (eds.), *Speech Genres and Other Late Essays* (trans. Vern W. McGee; Austin, TX: University of Texas Press, 1986), 103-31 (121-22).

In other words, Bakhtin believes that the speaker and the listener have a shared responsibility for both the formulation and reception of the message. This is because the fundamental unit of communication (whether oral or written) is the utterance, not the sentence. What distinguishes the two is that one can assume a responsive position only with respect to an utterance: 'one can agree or disagree with it, execute it, evaluate it and so on'.[103] Consequently, when a speaker prepares an utterance, whether it consists of a word, phrase, sentence or text, the speaker is always aware of an anticipated response, and thus frames the speech in terms of both the preceding utterance and the anticipated rejoinder. For this reason, as Gary Saul Morson and Caryl Emerson explain, it can be said that 'Bakhtin's dialogic model represents readers as shaping the utterance *as* it is being made', in contrast to reception theories that are 'usually concerned with how readers interpret texts *after* they are made'.[104]

The thoroughly dialogic nature of language, as conceived by Bakhtin, is most evident, however, when one considers the utterance itself: it is already filled with the words of others, which words 'carry with them their own expression, their own evaluative tone, which we assimilate, rework, and re-accentuate'.[105] The process of assimilation and re-accentuation, which is necessary if the utterance is to have meaning in new contexts, does not, however, suppress the memory of past meanings; rather, 'at certain moments of the dialogue's subsequent development along the way they are recalled and invigorated in renewed form (in a new context)'.[106] It

---

103. M.M. Bakhtin, 'The Problem of Speech Genres', in Caryl Emerson and Michael Holquist (eds.), *Speech Genres and Other Late Essays* (trans. Vern W. McGee; Austin, TX: University of Texas Press, 1986), 60-102 (74).

104. Gary Saul Morson and Caryl Emerson, *Mikhail Bakhtin: Creation of a Prosaics* (Stanford: Stanford University Press, 1990), 129 (emphasis in original). Iser, *The Act of Reading*, 21, also speaks of a shared responsibility—between text and reader—for transforming a text into a literary work, whose position is neither in the text nor the reader alone, but somewhere between the two. Consequently, Iser too finds the one-way model of communication inadequate: 'In literary works…the message is transmitted in two ways, in that the reader 'receives' it by composing it'. Iser's paradoxical formulation, however, does not appear to recognize the extent to which, according to Bakhtin's conception, the reader/hearer is involved in the very formulation of the text/utterance, not just in its subsequent actualization.

105. Bakhtin, 'Speech Genres', 89.

106. M.M. Bakhtin, 'Toward a Methodology for the Human Sciences', in Caryl Emerson and Michael Holquist (eds.), *Speech Genres and Other Late Essays* (trans. Vern W. McGee; Austin, TX: University of Texas Press, 1986), 159-72 (170).

is language dialogically conceived as an ongoing process of assimilation and re-accentuation of unique, historically-determined meanings that provides the theoretical basis for an alternative model of reading.[107]

Bakhtin himself once criticized the concept of a hypothetical reader—the ideal reader—as being nothing more than 'a mirror image of the author':

> [The ideal reader] cannot introduce anything of his own, anything new, into the ideally understood work or into the ideally complete plan of the author. He is in the same time and space as the author or, rather, like the author he is outside time and space (as is any abstract ideal formulation), and therefore he cannot be *an-other* or other for the author, he cannot have any *surplus* that is determined by this otherness.[108]

In this brief discussion of the ideal reader's limitations, Bakhtin is especially critical of the ideal reader's inability to contribute to the production of meaning.[109] As the author's mirror image, the ideal reader lacks the evaluative perspective that is constitutive of dialogic relations.

These notes of Bakhtin, written near the end of his life, represent a return to the subjects that had preoccupied him in his youth, in particular, the philosophical problem of self–other relations. In his early essay, 'Author and Hero in Aesthetic Activity',[110] Bakhtin views the problem of self–other relations in terms equivalent to the activity of an author creating a hero: just as an author creates a hero in a work of art, so an other creates a self in life. This is possible, as Michael Holquist explains, because for Bakhtin 'both activities are driven by a perceptual mandate to consummate'.[111] The same mandate lies behind the reader's encounter with the

107. See Shepherd, 'Theory of Reading', 137-43.

108. Bakhtin, 'Toward a Methodology', 165 (emphasis in original).

109. Iser, *The Act of Reading*, 28-29, also finds the concept of an ideal reader problematic: such a reader would have to share the author's underlying intentions, rendering communication superfluous.

110. M.M. Bakhtin, 'Author and Hero in Aesthetic Activity', in Michael Holquist and Vadim Liapunov (eds.), *Art and Answerability: Early Philosophical Essays by M.M. Bakhtin* (trans. and notes Vadim Liapunov; supplement trans. Kenneth Brostrom; Austin, TX: University of Texas Press, 1990), 4-256. According to Michael Holquist, 'Introduction: The Architectonics of Answerability', in Holquist and Liapunov (eds.), *Art and Answerability*, ix-xlix (xvii-xviii), the essay 'Author and Hero' is dated from 1920–23, the so-called philosophical period of Bakhtin's life, but did not appear until 1979.

111. Holquist, 'Introduction', xxx.

text, a type of co-authoring or re-authoring by which the reader 'transforms a text into an event by giving it meaning'.[112]

I have selected 'Author and Hero' as the principal theoretical work of the methodology section of this study, because the essay's central metaphor lends itself to a careful examination of reader–character interaction in Matthew's Gospel. Although it represents some of Bakhtin's earliest work, the importance of 'Author and Hero' is undoubted: according to Holquist 'it contains many, if not most, of the ideas [Bakhtin] would spend the rest of his life exploring, revising, or even contradicting'.[113] One of the goals of the methodology section of this study will be to relate Bakhtin's philosophical discussion to his subsequent thought on language as dialogic event.

112. Holquist, 'Introduction', xxxi.

113. Holquist, 'Introduction', xvii. Despite the severe hardships that Bakhtin was forced to endure, he saved the notebooks of the original manuscript his entire life, an indication of the value he attached to 'Author and Hero'. Holquist's characterization of Bakhtin's thought as an active, life-long exploration of certain themes is partly intended to underscore the point that Bakhtin's work is more about process than it is about result.

Chapter 2

METHODOLOGY

Bakhtin and the Project of Reading

Mikhail Bakhtin was not a theoretician of reading. As a matter of fact, he was critical of theories in general, inasmuch as they tended, in his view, to privilege either the general formulation or its specific data. It was for this reason, for example, that he criticized Saussure's model of language. According to Bakhtin, Saussure's distinction between *langue* and *parole* was responsible for creating the misconception that an utterance is merely the momentary concrete expression of the linguistic system, merely the ordered accumulation of linguistic units, such as words and sentences. Although there are indeed utterances that contain words and sentences, utterances, according to Bakhtin, are also constituted by elements outside of Saussure's *langue*, which is otherwise unable to account for them. The investigation of these elements became the goal of a new linguistics, which Bakhtin called metalinguistics.[1]

Bakhtin's rethinking of the nature of language and the discipline of linguistics was not intended, however, to replace one theory with another. Therefore, readers of Bakhtin who expect to find a systematic presentation of an overarching theory will be disappointed. For, as Holquist warns, Bakhtin's work 'can be called theoretical only in the sense that all grand *anti*-theories are inevitably implicated in what they oppose'.[2] Although the

---

1. For a discussion of metalinguistics, see Morson and Emerson, *Creation of a Prosaics*, 123-71. Bakhtin uses the term 'metalinguistics' in Mikhail Bakhtin, *Problems of Dostoevsky's Poetics* (ed. and trans. Caryl Emerson; Minneapolis: University of Minnesota Press, 1984), 202: 'Stylistics must be based not only, and even *not as much*, on linguistics as on *metalinguistics*, which studies the word not in a system of language and not in a 'text' excised from dialogic interaction, but precisely within the sphere of dialogic interaction itself, that is, in that sphere where discourse lives an authentic life' (emphasis in original).

2. Holquist, 'Introduction', xx.

sum of Bakhtin's correctives does not properly constitute a system, when these correctives are considered together with the theories that they oppose, it is possible to discern, if not a system, then at least an approach.

Broadly speaking, Bakhtin's work can be characterized, in Holquist's words, as 'the positing of problems in precisely the right measure of generality and specificity'.[3] In his early philosophical essays Bakhtin examines the problem of balance between generality and specificity as it pertains to an author's activity with respect to the hero of an aesthetic work, which activity assembles the disparate *parts* of a hero's forward-directed inner life into a unitary *whole* of meaning. The author's organizing role constitutes, for Bakhtin, the aesthetic moment proper.

The philosophical ground of Bakhtin's analysis of authoring is ultimately to be found in his understanding of self–other relations, which Bakhtin conceives as a potentially productive relationship of essentially non-coinciding perspectives. As Ann Jefferson explains, '[t]he relations between self and Other are viewed as equivalent to those between hero and author. This is because the self is always "authored" or created by the Other/author.'[4] This analysis, as well as Bakhtin's later work on language as dialogic event, has prompted some scholars to apply his insights to the project of reading.[5]

Although Bakhtin does not develop an overarching theory of reading, one nevertheless finds interspersed throughout his writings references to the role of readers in creating meaning, whether understood as the reader's contribution to the meaning of a text or the listener's contribution to the meaning of a speech act. From his early philosophical essays it becomes clear that Bakhtin conceives the reader's role as a type of authoring, albeit a secondary one, which he calls co-authoring or co-creating. Consequently, Bakhtin's analysis of the author's relationship to the hero of an aesthetic work outlines in principle his conception of the reader's approach to the hero as well.

3.   Holquist, 'Introduction', xx.

4.   Ann Jefferson, 'Bodymatters: Self and Other in Bakhtin, Sartre and Barthes', in Ken Hirschkop and David Shepherd (eds.), *Bakhtin and Cultural Theory* (Manchester: Manchester University Press, 1989), 152-77 (154).

5.   In biblical studies, for example, see Walter L. Reed, *Dialogues of the Word: The Bible as Literature According to Bakhtin* (New York: Oxford University Press, 1993); McCracken, 'Character in the Boundary', 29-42; David McCracken, *The Scandal of the Gospels* (New York: Oxford University Press, 1994); and Barbara Green, *Mikhail Bakhtin and Biblical Scholarship: An Introduction* (SBLSS; Atlanta: Society of Biblical Literature, 2000).

The purpose of the methodology section of this study is to present those aspects of Bakhtin's analysis of the author–hero relationship that would be useful for defining the role of the readers of Matthew's Gospel. The model of reading that I shall propose, however, is not derived solely from Bakhtin's analysis; rather, it is born of a dialogic encounter between Bakhtin's theory of aesthetics and contemporary approaches to Matthew's Gospel, an encounter very much like Bakhtin's response to the theories of his time.[6] Nevertheless, before beginning the discussion of Bakhtin's analysis, I should first address an apparent problem: the purpose of this study is to investigate the readers' interaction with Matthew's group characters, whereas Bakhtin's analysis describes the author's relationship with a single hero of an aesthetic work.

In one sense, the problem is unavoidable: Bakhtin's theory of aesthetics is rooted in his understanding of the philosophical problem of self–other relations, which essentially pre-determines the perspective and content of his analysis. On the other hand, however, the nature of Matthew's group characters is such that they are often virtually indistinguishable, with respect to their manner of characterization, from the narrative's individual characters: as Kingsbury observes, '[g]roups of persons, like the 'crowds', for example, may function as a single character'.[7] The fact that Matthew's group characters can be treated as a single character does not, however, completely resolve the problem: Matthew's group characters are also fragmentary characters, not the generally well-developed heroes of modern literature, who implicitly serve as the basis for Bakhtin's analysis.[8] Nevertheless, even though Bakhtin's analysis typically addresses the problem of the main character of an aesthetic work, it should become clear in the course of the presentation that this approach can be applied to any character, indeed, even inanimate objects or phenomena of nature, as attested

6. Similarly, Green, *Mikhail Bakhtin*, 58, who contends that 'the most fruitful use of Bakhtin involves not simply exegeting and explicating his work but developing it while simultaneously appropriating it—a project both compatible with all that Bakhtin represents and also undertaken by most Bakhtin scholars'.

7. Kingsbury, *Matthew as Story*, 9.

8. Green, *Mikhail Bakhtin*, 27, recognizes a similar problem regarding the possible anachronism of appropriating Bakhtin's ideas on Dostoevsky for ancient Hebrew prose. Nevertheless, she argues that biblical language can indeed be worked dialogically, '[s]ince Bakhtin came to the insight that it was the "novelness" of language (not just "novels" per se) that was of significance to his thought, and since he himself criticized theorists who did not see deeply enough' (60-61).

by Bakhtin's example of an aesthetic approach to a cliff.[9] Moreover, inasmuch as the role of the readers, as conceptualized by Bakhtin, is a type of secondary authoring whereby the readers are expected to re-assemble the scattered self-manifestations of the characters, the problem of fragmentation posed by Matthew's group characters may be more apparent than real.

Author and Hero in Aesthetic Activity

In his extended essay 'Author and Hero in Aesthetic Activity', Bakhtin seeks the proper understanding of an author's relationship to the hero of an aesthetic work. He begins the essay with the observation that in life we human beings 'react valuationally to every self-manifestation on the part of those around us'.[10] Like the author of a text, who 'intonates every particular and every trait of his hero', we human beings ascribe meaning and intention to the self-manifestations of other human beings.[11] Unlike the author of a text, however, these valuations on our part are fragmentary: we tend to react to the individual's isolated self-manifestations rather than to an all-encompassing definition of the person. Even when attempts are made to consider the whole of an individual, such as characterizing the individual as kind or vicious, these attempts represent not an encompassing definition but 'a prognosis of what we can and what we cannot expect from him'.[12] In other words, according to Bakhtin, in life we react not to the whole of an individual but to those parts of the individual's activity that are of special interest to us. It is only in a work of art, Bakhtin argues, that the self-manifestations of a human being are given a truly unitary character, in this case, as the self-manifestations of the hero of a work of art.[13]

The author of an aesthetic work, unlike human beings in life, 'assembles all of the cognitive-ethical determinations and valuations of the hero and consummates them in the form of a unitary and unique whole that is a

---

9.   Bakhtin, 'Author and Hero', 66-67.
10.   Bakhtin, 'Author and Hero', 4.
11.   Bakhtin, 'Author and Hero', 4.
12.   Bakhtin, 'Author and Hero', 5.
13.   This is not to say that an author is not also shaped by the author's own interests and will. Rather, as discussed below, the author of an aesthetic work is able to assemble all of the hero's self-manifestations, because, by definition, the author is the one who creates both the hero and the hero's self-manifestations.

concrete, intuitable whole, but also a whole of meaning'.[14] By assembling *all* of the hero's self-manifestations, the author overcomes the fragmentary nature of reactions that is typical of everyday life, which reactions are shaped by the observer's own needs and expectations. By *accepting* all of the hero's self-manifestations, whether good or evil, the author overcomes the ethical, volitional orientation of everyday life, again which orientation is shaped by the observer's own interests and will. This activity of the author with respect to the hero is called aesthetic contemplation. Although Bakhtin himself does not formally develop a model of aesthetic contemplation, it is possible to derive one from his discussion of the author's relationship to the hero.

Toward a Model of Aesthetic Contemplation
Briefly, the activity of aesthetic contemplation, as described by Bakhtin, is a two-step process, although the steps themselves are not necessarily sequential. First, the author projects himself or herself into the hero in order to co-experience the hero's inner life, in order to 'see [the hero's] world axiologically from within him as *he* sees this world'.[15] Moments that are transgredient to the hero, that are beyond the consciousness of the hero, are unavailable, during this step, to the author as well. Second, the author returns to his or her own place outside the hero in order to 'fill in' the hero's perspective by means of the knowledge that is in principle unavailable to the hero from within himself or herself, which knowledge Bakhtin calls the author's excess or surplus of seeing. Ultimately, the purpose of aesthetic contemplation is to 'enframe [the hero], create a consummating environment for him out of this excess of [the author's] own seeing, knowing, desiring, and feeling', thereby transposing the hero onto a new plane of existence, namely, the aesthetic plane.[16]

These preliminary remarks introduce the fundamental presuppositions of aesthetic contemplation, which are (1) the hero's noncoincidence or inability to organize completely and finally his or her own inner life; and

14. Bakhtin, 'Author and Hero', 5.
15. Bakhtin, 'Author and Hero', 25 (emphasis in original). 'Axiologically' and 'axiological' are Vadim Liapunov's translations of *tsennostno* and *tsennostnyj*, meaning 'with respect to value, relating to value, from the standpoint of value' (235 n. 25). Therefore, when Bakhtin speaks of an 'axiological approach' to the events of one's life, he means 'any emotional-volitional position that would give them meaning with respect to value' (104).
16. Bakhtin, 'Author and Hero', 25.

(2) the author's surplus of vision with respect to the hero, by which the author is able to assemble the hero's forward-directed inner life into a unitary whole of meaning. These preliminary remarks also suggest the difficulty of assigning such a role to anyone other than the author of an aesthetic work: only the author is able to adopt a truly encompassing, and at the same time non-judgmental, orientation toward another individual, in this case, the hero of the aesthetic work.

Hero's Noncoincidence

Bakhtin begins his discussion of aesthetic contemplation by establishing that it is impossible for an individual to consummate, or assemble into a whole of meaning, his or her own transgredient moments, those moments that are in principle beyond the range of the individual's knowledge. The most obvious examples of moments that are necessarily transgredient include both temporal and spatial moments, such as the individual's own birth and death, even the appearance of the individual framed against the sky. Not only are these moments beyond the range of the individual's knowledge, more importantly, they are beyond the range of the individual's ability to comprehend them as meaningful events of the individual's life. As Bakhtin explains, 'the point here is not merely the impossibility of experiencing these events in fact; the point is first of all that I lack an essential axiological approach to them'.[17] I lack an approach to these events that would enable me to experience them in their entirety as events of my own life; I lack, in other words, an 'emotional-volitional position that would give them meaning with respect to value'.[18] While it may be possible, for example, to imagine a world 'emotionally toned by the fact of my death, the fact of my nonexistence',[19] it is not possible to experience it. Therefore, my death is necessarily a transgredient moment of my forward-directed inner life.

One of the consequences of the inability to achieve an axiological approach to my death is that I therefore lack the necessary vantage point from which I could consummate, or assemble into a whole of meaning, all of the other moments of my life as well. As long as I live, my cognitive and ethical actions remain unconsummated moments that are oriented entirely 'within the open ethical event of [my] lived life or within the

---

17. Bakhtin, 'Author and Hero', 104.
18. Bakhtin, 'Author and Hero', 104.
19. Bakhtin, 'Author and Hero', 104.

projected world of cognition'.[20] While my own consciousness may be able to anticipate or imagine the consummation of these moments, only someone who is situated outside my perspective, which Bakhtin calls an individual's horizon, is able to contemplate and subsequently bring these and other transgredient moments together into a whole of meaning. My anticipation or imagination of these moments, moments by which the other would otherwise consummate my forward-directed inner life, actually deprives them of their consummating power. Rather than consummating the moments of my inner life, anticipation merely extends my limited horizon. This is because, as Bakhtin explains, 'this whole would not be able to take possession of us and really consummate us for ourselves: our consciousness would take that whole into account and would surmount it as just one of the moments in its own unity'.[21] Anticipated consummation is a misnomer, not only because the transgredient moments are merely surmounted rather than truly consummated, but because anticipated consummation represents a form of self-activity, 'not a unity that is *given* but a unity that is set as a *task*'.[22] Indeed, from the perspective of the open-endedness of a lived life, every action, whether ethical or cognitive, is by definition set as a task, as that which is not yet consummated. On the other hand, the whole of meaning that is characteristic of aesthetic contemplation is a unity that is given, a unity that is no longer open-ended, that is, a unity that is no longer set as a task.

This tension between that which is given and that which is set as a task expresses, for Bakhtin, the essential contradiction of the ethical moment, the contradiction of 'is' and 'ought', of being and obligation. According to Bakhtin,

> The future as future of meaning is hostile to the present and the past as to that which is devoid of meaning; hostile in the way a task is hostile to not-being-fulfilled-yet, or what-ought-to-be is hostile to what-is, or atonement is hostile to sin.[23]

One implication of such hostility is that my past and present are essentially annulled in favor of the future. Consequently, as Bakhtin argues,

> I do not accept my factually given being; I believe insanely and inexpressibly in my own noncoincidence with this inner giveness of myself. I cannot

20. Bakhtin, 'Author and Hero', 12.
21. Bakhtin, 'Author and Hero', 16.
22. Bakhtin, 'Author and Hero', 16 (emphasis in original).
23. Bakhtin, 'Author and Hero', 122.

count and add up all of myself, saying: this is *all* of me—there is *nothing more* anywhere else or in anything else; I already exist *in full*.[24]

According to Bakhtin, this noncoincidence is the unfortunate condition of all human beings, a condition resulting from our inability to consummate ourselves despite our need for such consummation. The impossibility of self-conscious consummation, therefore, makes it necessary that an other be positioned outside the self—both with respect to time and space. In other words, human beings need a consciousness whose vantage point encompasses all of the experiences of the self—the self's life and death, as well as the self's 'is' and 'ought'. In principle such a vantage point belongs to the other in life; it is achieved perfectly, however, only by the author of an aesthetic work with respect to the hero.

Author's Surplus

According to Bakhtin, the position of the author of an aesthetic work with respect to the hero is, by definition, 'an intently maintained position *outside* the hero with respect to every constituent feature of the hero—a position *outside* the hero with respect to space, time, value, and meaning'.[25] These transgredient features constitute the author's surplus of knowledge with respect to the hero, which knowledge is in principle inaccessible to the hero's consciousness.

From this position of surplus the author must assemble the hero's dispersed inner life, complete it 'by supplying all those moments which are inaccessible to the hero himself from within himself (such as a full outward image, an exterior, a background behind his back, his relation to the event of death and the absolute future, etc.)', and justify it 'independently of the meaning, the achievements, the outcome and success of the hero's own forward-directed life'.[26] As long as the activity of the author does not intrude on the consciousness of the hero, but remains transgredient to the hero's awareness, Bakhtin characterizes the event as aesthetic, rather than ethical or cognitive. On the other hand, should the consummating activity enter the consciousness of the hero and become simply another moment considered by the hero, it is surmounted by the hero's consciousness and deprived of its consummating force. In this case the aesthetic event comes to an end. Therefore, in order for the author to

---

24. Bakhtin, 'Author and Hero', 127 (emphasis in original).
25. Bakhtin, 'Author and Hero', 14 (emphasis in original).
26. Bakhtin, 'Author and Hero', 14.

actualize the relationship with the hero as an aesthetic relationship, the author must preserve the author's surplus of knowledge with respect to the hero. In other words, the author's consummating activity must be a form of contemplation. This explains why Bakhtin is not, as such, concerned 'with those actions which…are directed toward the actual modification of the event and of the other as a moment in that event; such actions are purely *ethical* actions or deeds'.[27] Rather, Bakhtin is concerned with consummation as an aesthetic activity. Such 'actions of contemplation do not go beyond the bounds of the other as given; they merely unify and order that given', a unity and an order that are apparent only to the author.[28]

Confessional Self-Accounting

As human beings, one consequence of our inability to assemble the dispersed moments of our forward-directed inner life is that we seek instead the consummated images of ourselves in the authoring activity of others. Although such images can never consummate us, inasmuch as they represent moments that are surmounted by our consciousness, it is possible that such images would evoke on our part a response that represents a type of self-objectification, which Bakhtin calls 'confessional self-accounting'.[29]

Bakhtin describes confessional self-accounting as a 'pure, axiologically solitary relationship to myself', which is achieved by 'overcoming all the transgredient moments of justification and valuation that are possible in the consciousness of other people'.[30] Although confessional self-accounting is an act that strives to overcome the consummating images on the part of others, which images would otherwise remain transgredient to self-consciousness, paradoxically it is an act that is possible only in community with others. This is because the act of confessional self-accounting is possible only in the presence of an other whom I consider to be authoritative for me, that other whose consummating image of me is able to provoke a penitential response on my part. In other words, confessional self-accounting is an act of potential self-determination consequent to ethical reflection. As Bakhtin explains,

27. Bakhtin, 'Author and Hero', 24 (emphasis in original). In this passage, because he is speaking from the perspective of the author, Bakhtin is referring to the hero, not the author, when he says that contemplation does not seek to modify 'the other'.

28. Bakhtin, 'Author and Hero', 24.

29. Bakhtin, 'Author and Hero', 141.

30. Bakhtin, 'Author and Hero', 142.

> When my act is regulated by the ought-to-be as such, when it evaluates its
> own objects immediately in the categories of good and evil...that is, when
> my act is a specifically ethical act, then my reflection upon it and my
> account of it start determining me as well and involve my own determinate-
> ness.[31]

If confessional self-accounting is only possible in the presence of an
authoritative other, then the question is, What constitutes the authoritative?
On the one hand, the authoritative can be, quite simply, that which is
acknowledged by one to be influential or powerful. Bakhtin, however,
defines the authoritative for purposes of confessional self-accounting more
specifically: it is that which is capable of determining one's self-understanding. In other words, as Bakhtin explains,

> What renders the other an *authoritative* and inwardly intelligible author of
> my life is the fact that this other is not *fabricated* by me for self-serving
> purposes, but represents an axiological force which I confirm in reality and
> which actually determines my life (like the axiological force of my mother
> that determines me in childhood).[32]

Unfortunately, Bakhtin does not explain what makes the other valued
and authoritative for one's life. Besides the obvious example of the
mother's authority vis-à-vis her child, one can only surmise that authority
is accorded to others for as many reasons as individuals admire, value, or
need one another. Bakhtin's example of a mother's authoritative relationship with her child does suggest, however, that a loving glance on the part
of the other must be present in order for the other to be an inwardly
determinative force for me. In any case, what constitutes a determinative
force in confessional self-accounting is clear: the authoritative other is not
merely acknowledged by me to be authoritative but is in fact responsible
for determining my life.

According to Bakhtin, the other is inwardly determinative for me,
however, only when the other's consummating image of me is met with a
penitential response on my part, a response of moral self-reflection.
Indeed, moral self-reflection is, in Bakhtin's view, the appropriate attitude
when one is faced with the contradiction between one's 'is' and 'ought'.
This is because, as Bakhtin explains,

> Moral self-reflection knows no given that is positive, no present-on-hand
> being that is intrinsically valuable, inasmuch as—from the standpoint of

---

31. Bakhtin, 'Author and Hero', 141.
32. Bakhtin, 'Author and Hero', 153 (emphasis in original).

that which is yet to be attained (the task to be accomplished)—any given is always something unworthy, something that ought not to be.[33]

A penitent tone by itself, however, 'does not produce a whole and aesthetically valid image of inner life'.[34] Rather, the penitent tone must meet the authoritative loving glance of the other, which affirms the 'is' of the aesthetic object,[35] thereby transposing it to a new axiological plane where growth in meaning is possible. This transposition is possible, in other words, only when the interior life of the aesthetic object is experienced 'actively in the category of *otherness*'.[36] This means that the contradiction between 'is' and 'ought', between being and obligation, which confronts the individual within the individual's self, is, in the category of otherness, no longer experienced as a hostile contradiction; rather in the authoring activity of the other, being and obligation 'are organically interconnected and exist on one and the same axiological plane'.[37] Nevertheless, these contradictory attitudes toward the same experience are, according to Bakhtin, appropriate, indeed necessary: 'What the other rightfully negates in himself, I rightfully affirm and preserve in him, and, in so doing, I give birth to his soul on a new axiological plane of being.'[38]

Aesthetic Contemplation and Expressive Aesthetics

Although Bakhtin holds that consummation, or the author's organizing activity, constitutes the aesthetic moment proper, aesthetic contemplation itself requires the author to co-experience the hero's inner life, indeed without which experience there can be no aesthetic contemplation. Therefore, Bakhtin develops his understanding of aesthetic contemplation dialogically with the important late nineteenth century German theory of aesthetics, which viewed aesthetic activity as the act of co-experiencing the inner state of an aesthetic object, whether a work of art, a phenomenon of nature, or a human being. Although this theory of aesthetics was expressed in a variety of forms, such as the aesthetics of empathy, the

33. Bakhtin, 'Author and Hero', 114.

34. Bakhtin, 'Author and Hero', 114.

35. By 'aesthetic object' Bakhtin simply means the one who is aesthetically contemplated by an other.

36. Bakhtin, 'Author and Hero', 120.

37. Bakhtin, 'Author and Hero', 120. In this passage Bakhtin is speaking from the perspective of the author, who rightly affirms what the other person—the self, in Bakhtin's terminology—rightly negates in himself or herself.

38. Bakhtin, 'Author and Hero', 129.

aesthetics of inner imitation and the aesthetics of play, Bakhtin analyzes the theory only in its purest, most general form, which he calls 'expressive aesthetics'.[39]

The fundamental principle of expressive aesthetics, as conceived by Bakhtin, holds that the form of an aesthetic object is the outward expression of the object's inner life, the outward expression of 'its emotional-volitional state and its directness from within itself'.[40] In turn, the form of the aesthetic object serves as the means by which one is able to co-experience the inner life of that object, thereby actualizing the proper goal of aesthetic activity as conceived by expressive aesthetics. Although the activity of co-experiencing the inner life of an aesthetic object is also a fundamental step of aesthetic contemplation, Bakhtin attacks the theory of expressive aesthetics for its failure to articulate, despite its intention, a properly aesthetic moment.

In the first place, as Bakhtin observes, '[e]mpathizing occurs in all dimensions of life, not just in aesthetic perception'.[41] He accuses the proponents of expressive aesthetics of failing to indicate 'those features which demarcate *aesthetic* co-experiencing from co-experiencing in general'.[42] This is because, in Bakhtin's view, expressive aesthetics in fact lacks a proper conception of form. Inasmuch as 'form does not consummate content (in the sense of the sum total of what has been internally co-experienced, empathized), but merely expresses it', expressive theory is unable to account for the whole of the aesthetic object.[43] As long as the funda-

---

39. Bakhtin's analysis of the author–hero relationship is not concerned with the techniques associated with co-experiencing; he merely affirms that 'co-experiencing of another being's inner life does occur' (62). A number of biblical texts appear to presuppose the possibility of reader identification or projection: when Joshua assembles the tribes and charges them to choose for Yahweh, he offers them the opportunity to become adopted children of the exodus tribe, thereby making the exodus experience of Ephraim their own as well (Josh. 24). This interpretation is supported by the alternation of the pronouns 'you' and 'they' when Joshua relates events that were only experienced by the previous generation. The alternation of pronouns encourages the people standing before Joshua to identify with those who experienced the exodus event. Another example of identification encouraged by context is evident in the response of the Pharisees upon hearing the parable of the vineyard: when Jesus finishes telling the parable, the Pharisees 'perceived that he was speaking about them' (Mt. 21.45).

40. Bakhtin, 'Author and Hero', 62.

41. Bakhtin, 'Author and Hero', 64.

42. Bakhtin, 'Author and Hero', 64 (emphasis in original).

43. Bakhtin, 'Author and Hero', 67.

mental principle of expressive aesthetics is defined as the activity of co-experiencing the object's inner life, whether real or fictitious, the theory lacks a truly aesthetic moment.

Bakhtin exposes the failure of expressive aesthetics to account for the whole of a work of art by analyzing its approach to da Vinci's painting, *The Last Supper*. Inasmuch as expressive aesthetics seeks to understand an aesthetic object from within the object itself, in the case of an object that consists of several figures, such as da Vinci's painting, one inevitably must privilege the parts of the object over its whole. For example, in order to be able to understand each of the painting's figures, as Bakhtin explains,

> I must empathize myself into each one of the participants, co-experience the inner state of each one of them, by starting from their 'expressive' outward expressedness. Passing from one figure to the other, I can, by co-experiencing, understand each figure taken separately.[44]

The problem with this approach, however, is that it does not account for the work's unitary whole of meaning, which cannot be experienced simply by adding up its co-experienced parts. The parts, in this case the emotional-volitional attitudes of each of the participants of the painting, are 'intensely individual', indeed, 'in a state of active contraposition to each other'.[45]

Therefore, according to Bakhtin, in order to be able to understand the whole of this complex event, one must seek 'a position outside each one of [the participants] as well as outside all of them taken together'.[46] Such a position, it is argued, belongs to the author of the aesthetic work.

Productive Co-experiencing

The proponents of expressive aesthetics are correct when they identify the author's position as the one that encompasses the whole of the aesthetic work. In accordance with the fundamental principle of expressive theory, this encompassing position is gained by co-experiencing the aesthetic work with its author: 'While each hero expresses only himself, the whole of a work is said to be the expression of the author.'[47] Once again, however, Bakhtin attacks expressive aesthetics, this time on the grounds that it fails to apply consistently its fundamental principle: 'Co-experi-

---

44. Bakhtin, 'Author and Hero', 65.
45. Bakhtin, 'Author and Hero', 65.
46. Bakhtin, 'Author and Hero', 65.
47. Bakhtin, 'Author and Hero', 65.

encing with the author, insofar as he has expressed himself in a given work, is not a co-experiencing of his inner life (his joy, anguish, desires, and strivings) in the same sense as our co-experiencing with the hero is.'[48] Rather, as Bakhtin insists, '[c]o-experiencing with the author is a sharing of the actively creative position he has assumed in relation to what is presented'.[49] It is precisely this sharing of the author's creative position on the part of the contemplator that constitutes for Bakhtin the aesthetic moment. In other words, '[t]he aesthetic whole is not something co-experienced, but something actively produced, both by the author and by the contemplator'.[50]

The essentially productive nature of aesthetic activity, properly understood, is especially apparent when one seeks an aesthetic approach to inanimate objects or phenomena of nature, as in Bakhtin's example of an aesthetic approach to a cliff. Since, according to Bakhtin, the necessary precondition of aesthetic activity is that the imaged objects be endowed with a forward-directed inner life, the first step of an aesthetic approach is to vivify the objects, 'make them into potential heroes—the bearers of a destiny'.[51] As in the case of expressive theory, an aesthetic approach would utilize an object's external image to establish its possible inner state. The external image of a cliff, for example, might express such inner states as 'stubbornness, pride, steadfastness, self-sufficiency, yearning, loneliness',[52] which inner states could be co-experienced by the contemplator.

Unlike expressive theory, however, a truly aesthetic approach would not consider co-experiencing the possible inner life of this vivified cliff as an adequate end. This is because a truly aesthetic approach does not seek simply to repeat the possible emotional-volitional attitude of the imaged cliff. Rather it would 'paint a picture or produce a poem or compose a myth (even if only in imagination) where the given phenomenon will become the hero of the event consummated around the hero'.[53] In other words, a truly aesthetic approach would seek a stable position outside the object's possible forward-directed life from which to assemble the disparate elements of that life into a unitary whole of meaning. The resulting

48. Bakhtin, 'Author and Hero', 65.
49. Bakhtin, 'Author and Hero', 65.
50. Bakhtin, 'Author and Hero', 67.
51. Bakhtin, 'Author and Hero', 66.
52. Bakhtin, 'Author and Hero', 66.
53. Bakhtin, 'Author and Hero', 66.

artistic whole, whether a poem or a painting of the cliff, will not only express the possible inner states of the cliff, its soul, 'but will also consummate this soul with values transgredient to its possible self-experience: aesthetic grace will be bestowed upon it—a lovingly merciful justification of its being that is impossible from within the soul itself'.[54]

Outsideness and the Hero

Not only does expressive theory fail to establish a stable position outside the imaged object, from which it would be possible to assemble the disparate elements into an aesthetic whole, it actually destroys the aesthetic whole whenever it is available. For example, in accordance with the fundamental principle of expressive aesthetics, a spectator of a theatrical production would be expected to relinquish the spectator's outside position with respect to the characters on stage in order to co-experience the inner life of the characters, in order to see the stage through the characters' eyes. The result, according to Bakhtin, is that there is no longer 'an author as an independent and effective participant in the event. The spectator has nothing to do with the author at the moment of co-experiencing, for he is wholly inside the heroes'.[55] When the spectator relinquishes the author's position, however, he or she relinquishes the one vantage point capable of encompassing the entirety of the event, of assembling the disparate elements of the event into a unitary whole of meaning. In other words, when the spectator, so to speak, crosses the footlights, he or she destroys the possibility of making the event an aesthetic one. Instead, the event begins to resemble the activity of playing, where the players enact an event of life for no purpose other than 'to experience that life as one of its participants'.[56]

What is common to both expressive aesthetics and the activity of playing is that the observer seeks the experience of the other's inner life, not as the inner life of another person, but as the observer's own inner life: 'In every case...we have to do with a relationship to one*self*, with an experience in the category of the *I*, and the values presented are invariably correlated with the *I*.'[57] In other words, in terms of the distinction between parts and whole, expressive aesthetics privileges the discrete self-manifes-

54. Bakhtin, 'Author and Hero', 66-67.
55. Bakhtin, 'Author and Hero', 73.
56. Bakhtin, 'Author and Hero', 74.
57. Bakhtin, 'Author and Hero', 64 (emphasis in original).

tations of the other person's inner forward-directed life over the unitary whole of meaning.

Outsideness and the Event of Life

An attitude that Bakhtin considers closer to his conception of aesthetic contemplation is that of the naive spectator of a theatrical production who attempted to warn the hero about an impending ambush. The spectator correctly assumed a stable position outside the hero,

> took into account those features which were transgredient to the hero's consciousness, and was prepared to utilize the privilege of his own outside position by coming to the aid of the hero where the hero himself, from his place, was powerless.[58]

The mistake of the naive spectator, from Bakhtin's perspective, was that he failed to assume an equally stable position outside the entire event as it was enacted on stage, which position would have enabled his activity to develop in an aesthetic direction rather than an ethical one. Instead, as Bakhtin explains, the spectator became a new participant:

> He stepped across the footlights and took up a position beside the hero on one and the same plane of life lived as a unitary and open ethical event, and, in so doing, he ceased to be an author/spectator and abolished the aesthetic event.[59]

From this example it is clear that Bakhtin's principal criticism of expressive aesthetics is that it collapses the essentially different perspectives of author and hero into one, thereby eliminating the possibility of establishing the event aesthetically. Although I may empathize into the hero and co-experience the hero's inner life, inasmuch as I exclude the hero's transgredient features, which are necessary for enriching the life of the hero, I experience the hero's life in the same categories as the hero does, merely repeating the hero's experience. By simply repeating the hero's experience I abdicate my necessarily productive role as author. And if there is no author present, neither can there be an aesthetic event. What we have instead is the 'closed circle of a single consciousness, of self-experience, and of a relationship to oneself'.[60] In this case, 'form does not consummate content (in the sense of the sum total of what has been

---

58. Bakhtin, 'Author and Hero', 78-79.
59. Bakhtin, 'Author and Hero', 79.
60. Bakhtin, 'Author and Hero', 80.

internally co-experienced, empathized), but merely expresses it'.[61] It is only when I maintain a stable position outside the hero, both with respect to the hero's forward-directed inner life and the event of being, that I am able to function as an author, bestowing form upon the hero from moments that are in principle transgredient to the hero's consciousness. The unity and order derived from such actions of contemplation recall the loving words of a mother for her infant, the words that:

> for the first time determine [the infant's] personality *from outside*, the words that *come to meet* his indistinct inner sensation of himself, giving it a form and name in which, for the first time, he finds himself and becomes aware of himself as a *something*.[62]

Sympathetic Co-experiencing

The image of a mother's loving words toward her infant captures for Bakhtin an important difference between expressive aesthetics and aesthetic contemplation. Expressive aesthetics, in accordance with its fundamental principle, seeks a pure co-experiencing of the inner life of an aesthetic object. The most important deviation from this principle on the part of the proponents of expressive aesthetics is a type of co-experiencing that is characterized as sympathetic or compassionate, which Bakhtin calls 'sympathetic co-experiencing'.

Sympathetic co-experiencing represents a departure from pure co-experiencing: unlike expressive aesthetics, which seeks to co-experience the inner life of an aesthetic object without transforming it, sympathetic co-experiencing 'radically alters the entire emotional-volitional structure of the hero's inward experience, imparting an entirely different coloring or tonality to it'.[63] According to Bakhtin:

> [t]he notion of sympathetic co-experiencing developed to its ultimate conclusion would destroy the 'expressive' principle at its very root and would bring us to the idea of aesthetic love and thus to a proper understanding of the author's position in relation to the hero.[64]

It might be argued that some element of sympathy is necessary in order to empathize into the inner states of an aesthetic object, for it is reasoned that we do not empathize into unsympathetic objects. Bakhtin insists,

61. Bakhtin, 'Author and Hero', 67.
62. Bakhtin, 'Author and Hero', 49-50 (emphasis in original).
63. Bakhtin, 'Author and Hero', 81.
64. Bakhtin, 'Author and Hero', 81.

however, that while sympathy can be one of the conditions for co-experiencing, it is neither the only condition nor even a necessary one. This is because sympathetic co-experiencing, insofar as it approaches aesthetic contemplation, 'means to experience that life in a form completely different from the form in which it was, or could have been, experienced by the *subiectum* of that life himself'.[65] On the other hand, the type of co-experiencing that seeks to merge with the co-experienced life represents, regardless of its intention, 'a falling away of the coefficient of sympathy, of love, and, consequently, of the form they produced as well'.[66]

That Bakhtin refers to form as a product of sympathetic co-experiencing clarifies the reason he considers this variety of expressive theory to be close to aesthetic contemplation. Ultimately, for Bakhtin, sympathetic co-experiencing and aesthetic contemplation both represent ways of relating to an object in such a manner as to unify the object's horizon with its environment, to unify the directedness of its inner life with those moments that are transgredient to that inner directedness. Even if one argues that the activity of co-experiencing, whether of the expressive or sympathetic variety, includes an element of introjection, that is, of ascribing 'those qualities which express our own attitude toward the object *to* that object itself as its own qualities',[67] nevertheless, it is sympathetic co-experiencing's loving attention to the entirety of the object that distinguishes it from expressive theory. Whereas expressive theory would give meaning to the exterior of a happily smiling man by ascribing joy as his inner state, sympathetic co-experiencing would encompass the whole of the man, his exterior no longer viewed merely as a moment toward co-experiencing his inner life.

A Model for Reading Matthew's Gospel

The methodology section of this study has presented aspects of Bakhtin's analysis of the author–hero relationship that would be useful for establishing a different approach to Matthew's Gospel, by reconceptualizing the reader's role as it is typically conceived by gospel critics, whether implicitly by redaction critics or explicitly by narrative and reader-response critics. The dialogic nature of Bakhtin's approach, however, which frustrates those who seek in Bakhtin a model or system for reading, does not

65. Bakhtin, 'Author and Hero', 82.
66. Bakhtin, 'Author and Hero', 82.
67. Bakhtin, 'Author and Hero', 81 (emphasis in original).

easily translate into a model for reading Matthew's Gospel. Aesthetic contemplation, properly speaking, is not a model for reading; rather it represents a corrective to theories of aesthetics that were popular in Bakhtin's time. For this reason, therefore, in order for aesthetic contemplation to be understood properly, it must be considered together with the theories of aesthetics that it opposes. Nevertheless, it is also true that one can discern certain defining principles of aesthetic contemplation that are relevant to the study of reader–character interaction in Matthew's Gospel. The relevance of Bakhtin's theory of aesthetics for the project of reading is postulated on his understanding that the reader's activity is itself a type of secondary authoring, which Bakhtin calls co-authoring or co-creating.

In summary, the necessarily productive nature of the author–hero relationship presupposes a situation of two noncoinciding perspectives. Bakhtin's criticism of expressive theory is that it collapses the noncoinciding perspectives into essentially one consciousness, thereby destroying the aesthetic event. The second presupposition of aesthetic contemplation is the principle that human beings in life—the model for heroes in aesthetic works—are unable to consummate their own transgredient moments. The inability of human beings to consummate their own transgredient moments establishes the possibility for an other/author to transpose the directedness of the self/hero's inner life onto the aesthetic plane. An absolute consciousness, on the other hand, one with 'nothing transgredient to itself, nothing situated outside itself and capable of delimiting it from outside', is impossible to aestheticize. When this consciousness is 'the encompassing consciousness of God, a religious event takes place (prayer, worship, ritual)'.[68]

The first step of aesthetic contemplation proper is for the author to project himself or herself into the hero in order to co-experience the hero's inner life with all of its limitations with respect to time and space. The second step is for the author to return to the author's position outside the hero, indeed outside the hero's entire event of being, thereby precluding an ethical or cognitive-emotional response that would otherwise abolish the aesthetic event. The resulting aesthetic contemplation transposes the hero to a new plane of existence, which is not a repetition of the hero's experience, but the justification of that life independent of its forward-directed meaning.

When these principles are applied dialogically to the problem of reader–character interaction in Matthew's Gospel, they suggest several modifi-

68. Bakhtin, 'Author and Hero', 22.

cations to the reading strategies as currently practiced by Matthean scholars.

A Conceptually Mixed Portrait

The inability of redaction critics to reconstruct conclusively Matthew's historical community does not mean that their reconstructions are of no use. What emerges from their work is a conceptually mixed portrait of an audience that the Gospel itself creates, rather than the description of Matthew's actual historical audience. Whether or not the historical author of Matthew's Gospel intended to address specific groups within his community, such as Christian antinomian heretics, is unprovable. On the other hand, it is commonly accepted that Matthew places a general emphasis on the law's abiding validity for the Church,[69] which suggests that at least some of his historical addressees questioned the law's status. Similarly, Gundry's contention that Matthew's community was a mixed body characterized by a growing coldness of love and intramural betrayal[70] is also unprovable. Nevertheless, the Gospel's admonitions to practice love and to refrain from judging others implies that at least some of Matthew's historical addressees needed to hear these admonitions, otherwise it is inconceivable, from a redaction-critical perspective, why these admonitions would have been included in the first place.

An alternative to reconstructing a plausible historical community as the intended audience is to conceive the interaction between the readers and the text in terms of a conceptually mixed narrative portrait that imposes itself on all readers. Certainly this is true of Matthew's contemporary readers, who, as Bakhtin would insist, share the responsibility with the evangelist for both the formulation and reception of the Gospel.[71] But it is also true of subsequent generations of historical readers: inasmuch as language, as conceived by Bakhtin, is a thoroughly dialogic phenomenon, the historical process of a text's assimilation and re-accentuation does not suppress the memory of past meanings. Consequently, as Bakhtin explains, 'at certain moments of the dialogue's subsequent development along the way [past meanings] are recalled and invigorated in renewed form (in a new context)'.[72] This makes it possible, for example, for Dan Via to argue that the apparent conceptual tensions among the discipleship roles in

---

69. See Barth, 'Matthew's Understanding of the Law', 159-64.
70. Gundry, 'A Responsive Evaluation', 66-67.
71. Bakhtin, 'The Problem of the Text', 121-22.
72. Bakhtin, 'Toward a Methodology', 170.

Matthew's Gospel are transformed into an existential tension for the disciple–reader as the disciple–reader is moved through the story:

> She experiences herself as under the command to forgive and to perform works of radical obedience in order not to be condemned in the judgment. But she also experiences herself as graced without regard for merit, one from whom faith and righteousness are evoked by a prior grace.[73]

Via's example of reader–character interaction presupposes the readers' identification with the discipleship role, which despite a certain amount of ambiguity is basically a positive one. Conceivably, this type of character identification, which essentially imposes the conceptually mixed role of discipleship on the readers, could be extended to include the negatively portrayed characters, such as the Pharisees, as well. In this case, the readers would experience themselves under judgment, rather than merely under the threat of judgment. The challenge of such a reading strategy is to define a mechanism for encouraging a type of reader–character interaction that would move the readers through *all* of the story's modes of existence. Such interaction is the intention of a reading approach that is based on Bakhtin's theory of aesthetics.

Character Transgredience and Reader Surplus

When gospel critics describe the interaction between the implied reader and the text, they typically emphasize the sequential-temporal dimension of reading, which can be described as a process of anticipation and retrospection. Although these critics occasionally make note of the affective side of the sequential-temporal dimension of reading, more often they analyze the way it communicates information and encourages acceptance of the author's values. According to this paradigm, special significance is attached to information that is provided at the beginning of the narrative. This information creates initial reader expectations, which guide the implied reader's apprehension of all subsequent material.

Actual gospel readers, however, do not seem to experience the reading process in the same way that the implied reader does. One possible explanation for the disjunction between the experience of actual readers and the theoretical responses of the implied reader is that the construct typically presupposes a first-time reader, whereas the evidence concerning the historical reception of Matthew's Gospel suggests that the actual

73. Via, *Self-Deception*, 110.

readers were (and are) already familiar with the story. Prior knowledge of the Gospel's plot and values makes it less likely that the actual readers would be, in Stephen Moore's words, 'frustrated, thwarted, discomfited, startled, challenged, puzzled, or enlightened'.[74] Despite this significant criticism of the first-time reader construct, it is nevertheless true that narrative sequence is an important aspect of the reading process, and therefore should be considered when analyzing the readers' interaction with the text. It is here that Bakhtin's analysis of the author–hero relationship proves especially useful.

The presupposition of aesthetic contemplation is that human beings in life are unable to assemble into a whole of meaning those moments that are in principle beyond the range of their knowledge and understanding. The most obvious examples are temporal moments, such as an individual's own birth and death, and spatial moments, such as the appearance of an individual framed against the sky. It is only the author, by virtue of the author's surplus of vision with respect to the hero's time and space, who is able to assemble the hero's inner life into a unitary whole of meaning. The author consummates the hero's inner life by an act of aesthetic contemplation, first co-experiencing the hero's inner life with all of its limitations with respect to time and space, and then returning to the author's position outside the entire event of being in order to assemble this life into a unitary whole of meaning.

The sequential-temporal dimension of reading, theorized by reader-response critics as the limitation of a first-time reader, in our model would instead find expression as the temporal-spatial limitation of Matthew's characters from within their own forward-directed inner lives. Among the moments that are in principle transgredient to the Gospel's characters are the narrator's commentary, which is by definition only available to the readers, and those moments that lie ahead of the characters along the temporal axis of the narrative, in particular, the crucifixion and resurrection of Jesus and the final judgment. The readers, on the other hand, especially the readers who are already familiar with the story, occupy a position outside the limited horizon of the characters, indeed outside the entire narrative. Therefore, in accordance with the principles of our model of aesthetic contemplation, the readers would be expected to assemble, in an act of re-authoring, the scattered self-manifestations of the characters from within the characters themselves and consummate them by supplying

74. Moore, *Literary Criticism and the Gospels*, 106.

their transgredient moments. By first co-experiencing the characters' limited horizon, which includes not only their words and deeds but also their thoughts and intentions, the readers are able from a position of surplus to fill in the characters' transgredient moments, thereby transposing the characters onto a new plane of existence, which the characters are not able to experience from within themselves.

Authorial Values and Sympathetic Co-experiencing
Reader-response critics also consider characterization to be an important means of encouraging readers to accept the author's value system. Positive characterizations, as in the case of the supplicants, encourage readers to identify with the characters and to accept their values; negative characterizations, as in the case of the Pharisees, encourage readers to repudiate the characters as well as their values. The mixed portrayal of the disciples, on the other hand, requires readers to discern the difference between the behavior of the disciples, which often falls short of Jesus' expectations, and the function of the disciples, which is to be the recipients of his teaching.

From these examples it is clear that reader-response critics practice a limited form of reader–character identification, whose goal, however, is quite different from the one espoused by the theorists of expressive aesthetics. For reader-response critics, the purpose of character identification is to accept the author's values, not to co-experience the forward-directed inner life of the characters. Although the goal of reader–character interaction as conceptualized by reader-response critics is different, reader-response critics nevertheless repeat the fundamental mistake of expressive aesthetics: they essentially collapse the noncoinciding perspectives of the character and the author/reader into one consciousness, in this case, that of the author whose values they are expected to affirm. Consequently, the readers never actually experience the limited horizon of the characters' forward-directed inner life, an experience that is essential, as it is argued in this study, if the readers are to be truly grasped through all of the story's modes of existence. Aesthetic contemplation, on the other hand, describes a type of identification that accepts the values of the hero, whether good or evil, for the purpose of co-experiencing the hero's inner life, not as a type of Romantic empathic identification, but as the assimilation of the hero's linguisticm structure, which is comprised of the hero's words, deeds, thoughts and intentions. Acceptance of the hero's values, however, does not signal the readers' endorsement of those values. Rather, the purpose of co-experiencing the hero's inner life is to see the world as the hero sees it, to experience the limitation of the hero's perspective, so that the readers might consummate that life with the hero's transgredient moments, thereby experiencing the hero's life in an entirely different key.

Even consummation of the hero's inner life, however, is not the final goal of this model of reading, but a means of actualizing the conceptually mixed portrait of Matthew's Gospel. Insofar as the readers of Matthew's Gospel already endorse the values of the Gospel, a presupposition of this study, the values are in principle authoritative for them. However, the Gospel's conceptually mixed portrait addresses readers who do not actualize those values, who are not finally determined by them. The tension between avowal and actualization is itself an expression of the relationship between the noncoinciding perspectives of the hero's forward-directed inner life and the author's surplus of vision. This relationship was later reconceptualized by Bakhtin as a type of inner dialogue between the internally persuasive speech of the self and the authoritative speech of the other.

Human Consciousness as Inner Dialogue

During his linguistic period, Bakhtin came to understand human consciousness, or in his words, 'the ideological becoming of a human being', essentially as a type of inner dialogue, a 'process of selectively assimilating the words of others'.[75] Indeed, one's own word, one's very apprehension of the world, Bakhtin believed, 'is gradually and slowly wrought out of others' words that have been acknowledged and assimilated'.[76]

Bakhtin begins his discussion of verbal assimilation by referring to the principal modes of appropriating and transmitting another's words as these modes are taught in the classroom: (1) reciting by heart; and (2) retelling in one's own words.[77] The former mode—reciting by heart—describes the problem of authoritative speech and its assimilation: memorized words remain the words of another, words that are, so to speak, contained within quotation marks, resisting recontextualization and assimilation. This is because the authoritative word does not elicit agreement from us, by persuading us internally; rather, it demands our unconditional allegiance.

75. M.M. Bakhtin, 'Discourse in the Novel', in Michael Holquist (ed.), *The Dialogic Imagination: Four Essays by M.M. Bakhtin* (trans. Caryl Emerson and Michael Holquist; Austin, TX: University of Texas Press, 1981), 259-422 (341).

76. Bakhtin, 'Discourse in the Novel', 345 n. 31.

77. Bakhtin, 'Discourse in the Novel', 341.

As Bakhtin explains,

> It enters our verbal consciousness as a compact and indivisible mass; one
> must either totally affirm it, or totally reject it. It is indissolubly fused with
> its authority—with political power, an institution, a person—and it stands
> and falls together with that authority.[78]

Inasmuch as its authority is ascribed by others, the authoritative word
remains alien to our ideological becoming. This is because, as Bakhtin
explains,

> The authoritative word is located in a distanced zone, organically connected
> with a past that is felt to be hierarchically higher. It is, so to speak, the word
> of the fathers. Its authority was already *acknowledged* in the past. It is a
> *prior* discourse. It is therefore not a question of choosing it from among
> other possible discourses that are its equal.[79]

The latter mode—retelling in one's own words—illustrates the process
by which another person's speech becomes internally persuasive, the condition in which words are no longer entirely alien, but have become 'half-
ours and half-someone else's'.[80] The internally persuasive word, therefore,
is never simply the verbatim repetition of another's word, which condition
is characteristic of authoritative discourse; rather, it is the creative appropriation of another's discourse, such that a new voice emerges:

> Its creativity and productiveness consist precisely in the fact that such a
> word awakens new and independent words, that it organizes masses of our
> words from within, and does not remain in an isolated and static condition.
> It is not so much interpreted by us as it is further, that is, freely, developed,
> applied to new material, new conditions; it enters into interanimating
> relationships with new contexts.[81]

The means by which the internally persuasive word awakens new and
independent words from within is by intensely interacting with other
internally persuasive words:

> Our ideological development is just such an intense struggle within us for
> hegemony among various available verbal and ideological points of view,
> approaches, directions and values. The semantic structure of an internally
> persuasive discourse is *not finite*, it is *open*; in each of the new contexts that
> dialogize it, this discourse is able to reveal ever newer *ways to mean*.[82]

78. Bakhtin, 'Discourse in the Novel', 343.
79. Bakhtin, 'Discourse in the Novel', 342 (emphasis in original).
80. Bakhtin, 'Discourse in the Novel', 345.
81. Bakhtin, 'Discourse in the Novel', 345-46.
82. Bakhtin, 'Discourse in the Novel', 346 (emphasis in original).

Normally the ideological process of an individual is characterized by a sharp gap between these two categories of discourse. Nevertheless, according to Bakhtin, despite their significant differences, 'the authority of discourse and its internal persuasiveness may be united in a single word— one that is *simultaneously* authoritative and internally persuasive'.[83] The convergence of authority and internal persuasiveness is rare, however; more often an individual's ideological consciousness is determined by the 'struggle and dialogic interrelationship of these categories of ideological discourse'.[84]

Bakhtin's discussion of speech categories represents not only a development in his thought but a complement to his analysis of the author–hero relationship. Consequently, the forward-directed inner life of the hero can also be described as an ideological consciousness that is constituted by the struggle of competing voices of authority and internal persuasiveness. Therefore, when Bakhtin's discussion of speech categories is applied to the problem of reader–character interaction in Matthew's Gospel, it also becomes possible to describe the forward-directed inner life of Matthew's readers themselves as an ideological consciousness of competing voices. While the narrative's various character groups, as we shall see below, are confronted by Jesus of Nazareth, challenging their understanding as well as their self-understanding, it is ultimately the readers of Matthew's Gospel who are challenged: they are addressed as imperfect disciples. The readers are challenged, however, not directly, but through their interaction with the narrative's major characters, the means by which they are grasped by the story's various modes of existence.

83. Bakhtin, 'Discourse in the Novel', 342 (emphasis in original).
84. Bakhtin, 'Discourse in the Novel', 342.

Chapter 3

JESUS OF NAZARETH

God's Supreme Agent

The most important character in Matthew's Gospel from a narrative-critical perspective is Jesus of Nazareth, inasmuch as he is the character who most influences the plot of Matthew's story. As Jack Kingsbury has observed, 'even when a babe in the infancy accounts the story revolves around him'.[1] More importantly, however, especially with respect to the problem of reader–character interaction, Matthew 'presents Jesus as God's supreme agent who is in complete accord with God's system of values'.[2] One implication of this portrayal of Jesus is that his attitude toward the other characters in the Gospel is determinative of the readers' response to these characters as well: the readers are expected to endorse or reject the values of the other characters depending on their response to Jesus and Jesus' appraisal of their response.

Although it is a common practice of gospel critics to categorize Matthew's characters, as either positive or negative, on the basis of their response to Jesus, it is David Howell's contention that no character group 'serves as the sole role model in its response to Jesus'.[3] This is primarily because no single character group perfectly embodies the teaching of Jesus. Therefore, as Howell correctly insists, the readers must learn from all of the Gospel's characters, both positive and negative, what it means to follow Jesus. On the other hand, it is also true that Jesus fully embodies his own teaching. Therefore, some scholars have concluded, despite certain qualifications, that Jesus himself serves as Matthew's model of discipleship.[4]

1. Kingsbury, *Matthew as Story*, 11.
2. Kingsbury, *Matthew as Story*, 11.
3. Howell, *Matthew's Inclusive Story*, 248, concurs with Anderson, 'Gender and Reading', 22-24.
4. Howell, *Matthew's Inclusive Story*, 248. See also Davies and Allison, *Matthew*, III, 707-18.

Jesus as Model of Discipleship

When the disciples, who are the principal recipients of Jesus' teaching, fail to embody completely the words of their teacher, presumably the need for a model of discipleship is established: the readers of Matthew's Gospel not only need the assurance that obedience is possible, that one can indeed actualize the teaching of Jesus, they also need examples of the type of obedience that they are expected to emulate. It follows, therefore, that the behavior of Jesus, which embodies his teaching, both confirms the possibility of obedience and establishes its form as well. In other words, the argument that Jesus is the model of discipleship for Matthew's readers is essentially rooted in the claim that Jesus is portrayed 'as a righteous person who knows and obediently does the will of God'.[5]

David Bauer's analysis of the structure of Matthew's Gospel would appear to confirm this interpretation. According to Bauer, one of the four major structural elements of the Gospel is Matthew's repeated comparison between Jesus and his disciples.[6] The areas of comparison include the mission of Jesus and that of the disciples, the ethical behavior of Jesus and the expected ethical behavior of the disciples, and the shared use of filial language. Once the links between Jesus and the disciples are recognized, Howell argues, the failure of the disciples to actualize Jesus' teaching in their own lives does not invalidate his teaching but encourages the readers to look to Jesus for the model of discipleship.[7]

Davies and Allison reach a similar conclusion from their redaction-critical perspective. Noting the many connections between the words and deeds of Jesus in Matthew's Gospel,[8] they conclude that Matthew, 'like

---

5.   Howell, *Matthew's Inclusive Story*, 251. Howell follows Jack Dean Kingsbury, *Jesus Christ in Matthew, Mark and Luke* (Philadelphia: Fortress Press, 1981), 74-75, who argues that the image of Jesus 'as the authoritative Son who knows and does his Father's will', which is established at his baptism and temptation, is subsequently confirmed in both the discourse and narrative sections of the Gospel: the discourses show that Jesus knows the Father's will, while the narrative portrays Jesus' obedience. Among the examples of the exemplary behavior of Jesus cited by Howell, 251-59, are Jesus' concern to do God's will (3.15; 4.4; 26.39, 42), his acceptance of the lowly role of Servant of God (8.17; 11.28-30; 12.18-21; 20.28), and his fulfillment of the law with acts of love, which include reception of children (19.13-15), association with sinners and outcasts (9.10-13; 26.6-13), and compassion for the people (9.36; 14.14; 15.32).

6.   Bauer, *The Structure of Matthew's Gospel*, 57-63.

7.   Howell, *Matthew's Inclusive Story*, 255-57.

8.   Davies and Allison, *Matthew*, III, 715-16. For example, Jesus exhorts others to be meek (5.5), because he himself is meek (11.29); he enjoins others to be merciful

Paul, Origen, and other early Christians, thought of Jesus as a model to be emulated'. Davies and Allison propose a social-historical explanation for Matthew's portrayal of Jesus as the model of discipleship: the undoubted historical crisis of Matthew's time and place of composition necessitated the presentation of an authoritative model for the purpose of adjudicating among competing claims. It is their contention that '[new] norms and authorities are always most persuasively presented when embodied in examples'.[9] Inasmuch as the early movement associated with Jesus represented such a new claim, it follows that 'Jesus himself, through the promulgation of the tradition about him, became the new model *par excellence*'.[10]

If one accepts the view that Matthew's Gospel is intended, at least in part, to establish the values of its readers, then the argument that Jesus is the model of discipleship is compelling. Although these values could conceivably be conveyed through Jesus' teaching alone, his deeds not only give expression to his words but also show him to be a person who does what he teaches,[11] which is itself an important aspect of his instruction: when Jesus attacks the Pharisees, it is partly because 'they preach, but do not practice' (23.3; cf. 12.36).

Despite the obvious strengths of this interpretation, however, there is an important criticism that can be made against it. As Howell himself concedes, Jesus functions on an entirely different level than the disciples: he is the object of faith (18.6); he is worshipped (14.33); he is the one whom God appoints to save his people from their sins (1.21); he calls disciples to follow him (4.18-20; 9.9); and he is the one who fulfills the law and the prophets (5.17).[12] In other words, Jesus:

> has a priority and uniqueness which cannot merely be imitated by his disciples, and sayings such as 14.31, 18.6 and 18.19-20 reflect the perspective

(5.7), because he himself is merciful (9.27); he demands faithfulness to the law (5.17-20), because he himself keeps the law (8.4); he teaches private prayer (6.6), because he himself prays alone (14.23); he commands others to take up their cross (16.24), because he takes up his (27.26). The examples could be multiplied.

9. Davies and Allison, *Matthew*, III, 713.

10. Davies and Allison, *Matthew*, III, 713.

11. The importance of congruity between word and deed is evident in the Hellenistic tradition, which, as Davies and Allison, *Matthew*, III, 711, point out, 'stressed the need for teachers to live as they taught'. Davies and Allison further speculate that the Hellenistic *topos* may have influenced Matthew's portrayal of Jesus.

12. Howell, *Matthew's Inclusive Story*, 257-58.

and idioms of the post-resurrection community who have experienced the presence of the risen Lord (28.20).[13]

Nevertheless, Howell defends the thesis that Jesus is exemplary of discipleship by appealing to the closing pericope (28.19-20), which, he insists, 'has the effect of stressing the continuing validity and binding character of the earthly Jesus' teaching and deeds for the Matthean community'.[14] Although the closing pericope in fact emphasizes only the teaching of Jesus (28.20), his deeds cannot be separated from his teaching: it is the behavior of Jesus—his life of model obedience—that 'helps give specific content to the moral and ethical expectations placed upon the disciples'.[15] Even though Jesus' behavior, in Howell's words, represents 'a perfect model to which the disciples will never attain',[16] the disciples' failure to be fully obedient to Jesus does not invalidate the perfect model: ultimately, the function of this model is to encourage real readers to judge and correct themselves, which process begins, according to Howell, when real readers assume the role of the implied reader, who is manipulated by the Gospel's narrative rhetoric.[17]

Although Howell correctly insists on the close connection between Jesus' words and deeds, he does not, however, adequately address the problem that Jesus' uniqueness presents for the readers' response to the characterization of Jesus. While it is certainly true that readers are able to use the ethical perfection of Jesus for emulation and self-correction, the concept of his uniqueness includes much more than his exemplary ethical behavior. By failing to address the other aspects of Jesus' uniqueness, Howell implies, perhaps inadvertently, that it is Jesus' ethical behavior that is ultimately normative for the disciples, and therefore, the readers of Matthew's Gospel.

If my reading of Howell is correct, then it appears that he has left a number of important questions unanswered: What does it mean for me to imitate the ethical behavior of God's Son, the object of my faith? Does my ethical behavior fulfill the law and the prophets? Does my ethical behavior save me from my sins?[18] Regardless of how one answers these particular

13. Howell, *Matthew's Inclusive Story*, 257-58.
14. Howell, *Matthew's Inclusive Story*, 258.
15. Howell, *Matthew's Inclusive Story*, 258.
16. Howell, *Matthew's Inclusive Story*, 258.
17. Howell, *Matthew's Inclusive Story*, 247. So also, Anderson, 'Gender and Reading', 24.
18. Davies and Allison, *Matthew*, III, 713-14, argue that the emulation of Jesus'

questions, there still remains the technical problem of how exactly the behavior of Jesus is exemplary for the readers. Although Howell does not explain the mechanism of emulation (and self-correction), it would undoubtedly involve some form of reader–character interaction, which Howell unfortunately does not analyze.

Despite its shortcomings, however, the thesis that Jesus is exemplary for discipleship offers a persuasive explanation for Matthew's portrayal of Jesus as the one whose words and deeds are consistent, especially in light of the disciples' failure to actualize Jesus' teaching. Therefore, an alternative interpretation of the role of Jesus, one that is based on Bakhtin's analysis of the author-hero relationship in aesthetic activity, must also be able to explain the relationship between the words and deeds of Jesus.

Words and Deeds

It has been argued by Howell that the ethical behavior of Jesus gives specific content to his teaching.[19] Matthew's portrayal of Jesus' ethical behavior, however, does not encompass the entirety of his deeds: as Howell acknowledges, Jesus is also the one who, among other things, saves his people from their sins (1.21).[20] But if salvation from sins is effected by Jesus' death on the cross (20.28; 26.28), then it is possible to argue that his death has a certain priority over his ethical actions, at least with respect to the matter of salvation from sins. Does this mean, then, that the role of his saving death and emulation of his ethical behavior are somehow in tension with one another? Clearly, the importance of this question for the problem of reader–character interaction is such that any discussion about the relationship between Jesus' words and deeds must also account for the role of his saving death, a unique aspect of his char-acterization.

Dan Via, in his analysis of structure and Christology in Matthew's Gospel, has proposed that a similarly tensive relationship—one between law and Christology—need not be viewed as a relationship of opposing

ethical behavior need not undermine his unique status as savior: clearly Jesus is presented in Matthew's Gospel as much more than an example of a human hero. On the other hand, to reject completely the notion of Jesus as an ethical model is, according to Davies and Allison, to undermine Matthew's portrayal of Jesus as a real human being.

19. Howell, *Matthew's Inclusive Story*, 258.
20. Howell, *Matthew's Inclusive Story*, 257.

themes, if one approaches the problem from the perspective of the Gospel's structure.[21] Via argues that inasmuch as a five-part law division[22] and a three-part Christology division[23] are both present as structural patterns in Matthew's Gospel, it is not necessary to choose one pattern over the other as the Gospel's overall structure, but to recognize that one pattern is foregrounded and the other is backgrounded. The foregrounded pattern, according to Via, is the three-part christological division; the backgrounded one is the five-part law division. As Via notes, however, law is not as backgrounded as an opposition between the two might suggest: while the narrative's Christology is the Gospel's more prominent content, the more prominent structure is the five-part division. The proper interpretation, therefore, is that through his sacrificial death—the Gospel's christological content—Jesus fulfills the law; he does not abolish it. His death resolves the tension between law and Christology, inasmuch as it fulfills the covenant of Jeremiah, offering the forgiveness of sins and the promise that God's law would be written upon the heart (Jer. 31.33-34). According to Via, the significance of the covenant of Jeremiah is that it ties together forgiveness and doing the law: forgiveness comes only through the sacrificial death of Jesus; the law is the law reinterpreted by Jesus in light of the love commandment.

One way, therefore, to account for Jesus' unique characterization—his saving death—is to conceptualize the relationship between Jesus' words and deeds as a relationship between law and Christology, but with Jesus' teaching and *ethical* deeds corresponding to law and his sacrificial death corresponding to Christology. One of the consequences of defining the correlations in this way is that Jesus' words and ethical deeds are

21. Dan O. Via Jr, 'Structure, Christology, and Ethics in Matthew', in R. Spencer (ed.), *Orientation by Dissertation* (Pittsburgh: Pickwick, 1980), 199-215 (210-13).

22. See Benjamin W. Bacon, *Studies in Matthew* (New York: Henry Holt, 1930), who conceived the five-part division of Matthew's Gospel, based on the repeated formula, 'And it happened when Jesus finished' (7.28; 11.1; 13.53; 19.1; 26.1). Bacon concludes that Matthew added 'large amounts of teaching material' and grouped it together into five discourses, apparently imitating the alternating narrative-discourse pattern of the Pentateuch (80-82).

23. See Jack Dean Kingsbury, *Matthew: Structure, Christology, Kingdom* (Philadelphia: Fortress Press, 1975), 1-39. Kingsbury remains the strongest advocate of a three-part division of Matthew's Gospel based on the formulaic statement, 'From that time Jesus began' (4.17; 16.21). When 4.17 and 16.21, together with 1.1, are recognized to be superscriptions that summarize the material that follows, the three-part structural pattern is said to present Jesus as Son of God.

transferred to the law side of the relationship as the two sides of the same coin: if Jesus' commandments represent the law reinterpreted in light of the love commandment, then his ethical deeds represent the actualization of the reinterpreted law (5.17-20). Inasmuch as it is ultimately the death of Jesus that fulfills the law, however, rather than his teaching or his ethical deeds, this suggests that Jesus' words and deeds are intended instead to express the implications of his sacrificial death for the readers of Matthew's Gospel. In other words, if Jesus is the one who fulfills the law, the same cannot be said of others, even though, according to Matthew, it is possible for them to keep the commandments (19.20).

The possibility that (apparently) good deeds might originate from an unredeemed heart, as Via has shown,[24] argues in favor of the interpretation that the readers of Matthew's Gospel are expected to do more than emulate the ethical behavior of Jesus, even if they do manage to correct themselves in the process: only insofar as Matthew's readers actualize the death of Jesus, only to the extent that they appropriate 'as the shape of [their] own existence the story of Jesus' death and resurrection',[25] can it be said that his death is indeed salvific for them. Consequently, the words of Jesus and the words about Jesus, which include the words about his saving death, must first redeem the heart of Matthew's readers, rather than simply present them with a model of discipleship that they are expected to emulate.[26] It is the contention of this study that Matthew's redemption of the heart, the seat of human understanding and intention, is offered as a possibility to the readers of Matthew's Gospel through their interaction with the character Jesus of Nazareth, as the interaction is conceived by Bakhtin's theory of aesthetic contemplation.

Jesus as Authoring Hero

Although Jesus of Nazareth is clearly portrayed as a character in Matthew's Gospel, he is, as many gospel critics have noted, a unique character.

---

24. Via, *Self-Deception*, 79-80, 89-90.

25. Via, *Self-Deception*, 122.

26. Via, *Self-Deception*, 122, argues that Jesus' death is saving because, as story, it releases people from their blindness—blindness to their flawed internal condition, blindness to what they might become, blindness to how God is dealing with their situation. The death of Jesus graciously renews the heart, paradoxically enabling the exceeding righteousness necessary for salvation but conferring forgiveness should that righteousness not be achieved (135).

The uniqueness of Jesus, however, extends beyond his role as God's supreme agent, beyond his characterization as the one who is worshipped (14.33), who saves his people from their sins (1.21), who fulfills the law and the prophets (5.17). Unlike the other characters in Matthew's Gospel, Jesus is also presented as the one who knows more than any of the other characters: he knows the thoughts of other characters (9.4; 12.25) and he knows the future, both his own (9.15; 16.21; 17.22-23; 20.18-19; 26.2) and that of others (8.11-12; 10.17-23; 11.22-24; 16.28; 19.28-30; 20.23; 24.2-44; 26.13, 21, 31-34). More importantly, however, especially with respect to the problem of reader–character interaction in aesthetic activity, Jesus is also able to occupy a position entirely outside his life: he is able to perceive his own life as the life of an other. This characteristic of Jesus represents a significant problem for the activity of aesthetic contemplation, the method of reader–character interaction developed in this study.

According to Bakhtin, an aesthetic event presupposes, on the one hand, a relationship of two noncoinciding perspectives and, on the other, the principle that human beings are incapable of consummating their own transgredient moments. Essentially, both presuppositions seek to preserve the notion of surplus, that which, according to Bakhtin, makes it possible to define an event as aesthetic. Therefore, aesthetic theories that collapse the noncoinciding perspectives into essentially one consciousness, such as the various forms of expressive aesthetics analyzed by Bakhtin in 'Author and Hero in Aesthetic Activity', destroy the aesthetic event by abandoning the position of surplus. Equally problematic for this theory is an absolute consciousness that has nothing transgredient to itself, which consciousness is by definition impossible to aestheticize, because it lacks a position of surplus. When the absolute consciousness, for example, is 'the encompassing consciousness of God', the event of two noncoinciding perspectives, according to Bakhtin, is no longer an aesthetic event, but a religious one, in which case, the appropriate form of response is prayer, worship, ritual.[27] On the other hand, a theory of aesthetics that establishes and maintains a position of surplus creates the possibility for an 'author' to transpose a 'hero's' inner life onto the aesthetic plane.

It is with respect to the matter of authorial surplus that Jesus' unique characteristics present a problem. Matthew's portrayal of Jesus, which is unquestionably the narrative portrayal of a character, nevertheless in certain respects appears to coincide remarkably with Bakhtin's definition

---

27. Bakhtin, 'Author and Hero', 22.

of a hypothetical absolute consciousness. Such a consciousness not only has nothing transgredient to itself, but is also able to consummate the transgredient moments of others. Like the author of an aesthetic work, Jesus is able to assemble all of the self-manifestations of the other characters, whether the self-manifestations are good or evil, thereby creating an all-encompassing definition of those characters. In other words, from his unusual perspective within Matthew's Gospel, Jesus of Nazareth is at the same time able to function as a character in the narrative world and the 'author' of an aesthetic work. The remainder of this chapter will examine the proposal that Jesus represents an 'aestheticized' absolute consciousness[28] and consider the implications of this representation for the problem of reader–character interaction in Matthew's Gospel.

Jesus as 'Aestheticized' Absolute Consciousness
The most important challenge to the proposal that Jesus of Nazareth represents an absolute consciousness is that his birth and death, which are in principle events beyond one's consciousness, are transgredient moments for him as well. And indeed, the opening narrative section of Matthew's Gospel relates events that happen prior to the birth of Jesus (1.18-25), none of which are subsequently reported to enter the consciousness of the adult Jesus. Even certain events immediately subsequent to his birth, such as Herod's inquiry regarding the birth place of the Christ (2.1-6), the flight to Egypt (2.13-15), the slaughter of the innocents (2.16-18), and the journey to Nazareth (2.19-23), also appear to be transgredient to Jesus' consciousness. As it turns out, however, these events are in fact entirely available not only to the consciousness of Jesus but to anyone who knows how to search the Scriptures. This interpretation is supported by Matthew's frequent use of scriptural allusions in the opening chapters: the allusions inform the readers that the events surrounding the birth of Jesus are the fulfillment of 'what the Lord had spoken by the prophet' (1.22; 2.15, 17, 23).

Mere knowledge of transgredient moments, however, is not sufficient for an individual to consummate his or her own forward-directed inner life. As Bakhtin explains,

28. The characterization of Jesus as an 'aestheticized' absolute consciousness, although a significant modification of Bakhtin's concept, represents an attempt to capture the tension in Matthew's portrayal of Jesus: on the one hand, Jesus is worshiped (14.33; 28.9, 17), Bakhtin's response before the encompassing consciousness of God; on the other hand, Jesus refers all things to his Father (4.4, 7, 10; 5.16; 6.6; 7.21; 10.32-33; 11.27; 24.36; 26.39, 42), the one truly absolute consciousness.

> Even if we succeeded in encompassing the whole of our consciousness as
> consummated in the other, this whole would not be able to take possession
> of us and really consummate us for ourselves: our consciousness would
> take that whole into account and would surmount it as just one of the
> moments in its own unity.[29]

What is still lacking, in other words, on the part of those who can search
the Scriptures, such as the chief priests and scribes who are asked where
the Christ is to be born (2.4-6), is an essential axiological approach to the
entirety of their lives. This is because, as Bakhtin insists, there is a fundamental difference between how one values the events of one's own life
and how others value those same events: only another person can experience a world that is emotionally toned by the anticipation of my birth, only
another person can experience my birth in its entirety as an event of his or
her life.

Jesus, on the other hand, is portrayed by Matthew as the one who is
perfectly attuned to the will of God (4.4; 7.21; 26.39, 42), which is expressed in the Scriptures. Therefore, through the perspective of the Scriptures Jesus is able to experience the world as colored by the anticipation of
his own birth: when the Holy Spirit informs Joseph in a dream prior to the
birth of Jesus that 'he will save his people from their sins' (1.20-21), it is
subsequently shown that Jesus understands the significance of his birth.
Indeed, it becomes apparent that the meaning of his birth informs the
entirety of his life: Jesus understands that his mission is to call sinners
(9.13), that his life is to be a ransom for many (20.28), and that forgiveness is to be effected by his death (26.28). In other words, it is not simply
that his birth and the events surrounding it are shown to be available to his
consciousness, but that he is able to assume an axiological approach to
events that should otherwise have been transgredient to his consciousness:
the significance of these events is actually shown to be constitutive of his
own self-understanding.

The death of Jesus, on the other hand, is clearly depicted by Matthew as
an event experienced in its entirety by the consciousness of Jesus. This is
attested primarily by Matthew's post-resurrection narrative: not only does
Jesus appear to his disciples after his death (28.9-10, 16-20), thereby
experiencing a world colored by his non-existence, a mixture of fear (28.8,
10), great joy (28.8) and doubt (28.17), but he promises to be with them
always (28.20). This recalls an earlier promise that 'where two or three are
gathered in my name, there am I in the midst of them' (18.20). Even if one

29. Bakhtin, 'Author and Hero', 16.

were to discount the latter references as allusions to a beloved memory, the post-resurrection appearance itself is sufficient evidence that Jesus is able to occupy a position beyond his death.

The significance of overcoming the limitation that is in principle imposed by one's death, as well as the limitation of one's birth, is not measured merely in terms of knowledge or imagination, both of which can normally be surmounted by one's own consciousness. Rather, the position beyond death is significant inasmuch as it affords one an emotional-volitional position from which to approach one's entire life. The fact that Jesus knows beforehand the circumstances of his death, which he describes in detail to his disciples (20.18-19), is not sufficient evidence of an axiological approach to his life. However, insofar as the detailed foreknowledge of his death functions as an indication that his death is voluntary, then the passion predictions do indeed support the contention that Jesus attains an encompassing axiological approach to his death, and therefore, to his entire life. This conclusion is supported by Matthew's portrayal of Jesus as the one who understands that his death is the will of God (16.23), that his death is necessary in order to fulfill the Scriptures (26.54-56).

Additional evidence that Jesus occupies a position outside his life is his use of the title 'Son of man', which Jesus frequently adopts as a form of self-reference when he speaks about his passion (17.9-12, 22; 20.17-19, 28; 26.1-2, 24, 45).[30] Apart from the theological significance of Jesus' self-designation, it serves to place his life's work, as colored by his voluntary death, entirely within the range of his own consciousness. In another example—the parable of the last judgment, in which the 'Son of man' returns as the eschatological judge (25.31-46)—Jesus again demonstrates that he occupies a position beyond his death yet within the range of his consciousness. In other words, by means of these 'Son of man' references Jesus shows that he occupies a position outside the events of his own life, a position of absolute consciousness, which in principle has nothing transgredient to itself.

Inasmuch as an absolute consciousness is by definition impossible to aestheticize, the activity of aesthetic contemplation cannot apply to an absolute consciousness in the same way that it does to those for whom there are transgredient moments. On the other hand, Jesus is clearly

---

30. Although Jesus does not use the title 'Son of man' in his first passion prediction (16.21), the context of the prediction refers to the Son of man (16.13, 27-28), the latter reference implicitly linking the passion to the glorious coming of the Son of man (10.23; 19.28; 24.30-31, 37, 39, 44; 25.31; 26.64).

presented as a character in Matthew's Gospel, who is ultimately bound, as are all characters, by the limitations of narrative art. Apart from the technical limitations imposed by the rules of narrative, however, there are other indications that Jesus is ultimately an aestheticized character, albeit one who is uniquely able to occupy a position outside the events of his life.

The first evidence of limitation is that Jesus does not know the time of the eschatological future (24.36), although paradoxically he is able to describe the events of that future (24.24-31). The second is that Jesus feels abandoned on the cross (27.46), despite his apparent knowledge that he is God's Son (11.27) and the certainty that he will be raised up (16.21; 26.32). In both instances, however, the limitation of Jesus is arguably the expression of his relationship with God, the one truly absolute consciousness. The fact that others, whether the disciples (14.28; 16.16), the centurion (27.54), or even the author Matthew (1.22-23; 3.16-17; 11.27; 17.5), know what Jesus himself does not seem to know on the cross could be construed as a limitation of Jesus' absolute knowledge, a moment transgredient to his consciousness. Alternatively, in light of the other indications of Jesus' self-knowledge, this apparent limitation could also be interpreted as a limitation characteristic of Jesus' relationship with his Father, rather than as a transgredient moment in Jesus' relationship with others: the knowledge that Jesus is God's Son is actually a knowledge that belongs only to God, which God himself chooses to reveal to others (11.27; 16.17). Furthermore, the likelihood of misunderstanding this revealed knowledge, as Peter does at Caesarea Philippi (16.21-23), argues against the interpretation that it is surely transgredient to Jesus' consciousness: unless one understands the nature of his voluntary death, then the declaration that Jesus is God's son is inadequate. The centurion's confession (27.54), on the other hand, because it takes place at the cross, represents the true actualization of God's revelation. Inasmuch as Jesus' self-understanding is colored by his voluntary death, however, the centurion's confession need not be characterized as a transgredient moment.

Regardless of how one finally interprets these apparent limitations of Jesus' absolute knowledge, it remains true that the character Jesus of Nazareth is still portrayed as an encompassing consciousness, who is uniquely able to assemble the self-manifestations of others, as well as his own self-manifestations, into a unitary whole of meaning.

Jesus as Encompassing Other

A survey of the other characters in Matthew's Gospel would show them to be typical characters incapable of consummating their own transgredient moments. The impossibility of self-conscious consummation, therefore, makes it necessary that someone be positioned outside the characters in order to encompass all of their experiences—life and death, but especially the contradiction of 'what is' and 'what ought to be'. Such a vantage point belongs, of course, to the author of Matthew's Gospel, who is clearly positioned outside the entirety of the aesthetic object, his text. In the case of Jesus of Nazareth, however, we encounter a hero for whom there are essentially no transgredient moments, a hero who is able to occupy a position outside the plotted world of Matthew's Gospel, yet ultimately within the boundaries of the text. This means that Jesus occupies a position similar to that of the author with respect to the other characters of Matthew's Gospel. In other words, this means that Jesus is able to function as both hero and potential 'author' of an aesthetic work.

In the same way that Jesus occupies a position outside the events of his own life, he establishes a similar position with respect to the events in the lives of the other characters: as an 'author' he encompasses and consummates their forward-directed lives with their transgredient moments. One way he does this is by 'knowing their thoughts' (12.25). Another way is by seeing their future, as in the examples of Judas's betrayal (26.21) and Peter's denial (26.30-35). It is particularly interesting to note that on certain of these occasions the hearers do not respond to Jesus' knowledge of their future (10.16-23), which suggests that these transgredient moments remain beyond their consciousness.

Even when the other characters respond to Jesus' encompassing words, however, the nature of their response sometimes shows that they do not, in fact, understand his words, again preserving these moments as essentially transgredient for them. For example, when the mother of the sons of Zebedee asks Jesus to place her sons in the positions of honor in his kingdom, he responds by referring to their participation in his future suffering:

> But Jesus answered, 'You do not know what you are asking. Are you able to drink the cup that I am to drink?' [The sons] said to him, 'We are able'. He said to them, 'You will drink my cup, but to sit at my right hand and at my left is not mine to grant, but it is for those for whom it has been prepared by my Father' (20.22-23).

The reaction of the other disciples, however, is directed against the brothers, which suggests that these words of Jesus have no meaning for them: 'And when the ten heard it, they were indignant at the two brothers' (20.24). In other words, the absence of an understanding response on the part of the disciples suggests that these words of Jesus remain a productive force only in the consciousness of Jesus, the observer, who co-experiences the inner life of the disciples in a tone that is otherwise unavailable to them. The readers, on the other hand, who co-author this encounter with Jesus, experience the disciples' limited perspective against the new context established by Jesus.

When the transgredient moments of others are consummated only in the consciousness of the observer, then the resulting consummation is considered to be aesthetic contemplation rather than ethical activity.[31] But in order for aesthetic contemplation to be truly productive as aesthetic activity, it must assemble all of the hero's self-manifestations; it must, in other words, be a loving contemplation, a type of contemplation that transposes its object onto a new axiological plane precisely because it does not selectively assemble the object's self-manifestations for self-serving purposes. Although the transposition onto a new axiological plane occurs only in the eye of the beholder, nevertheless, it still effects a new birth, literally bringing into existence something that did not previously exist, even if only in the eye of the beholder. For example, when an unnamed woman anoints Jesus with an expensive ointment, it is only Jesus who sees her action toward him as 'a beautiful thing'; the others criticize her for neglecting the poor (26.6-13). Ironically, the gesture is indeed extravagant. Only someone who is situated entirely outside the events of Jesus' life, namely, Jesus himself, could possibly see this as a proleptic burial preparation. Jesus' position of outsideness with respect to his own life enables him to transpose the unnamed woman's action toward him onto a new plane of meaning, which is informed by his voluntary death. When Jesus explains the meaning of her action to the disciples, once again they do not respond: Jesus' loving transposition apparently remains transgredient to their consciousness.

---

31. Bakhtin's definition of aesthetic contemplation is not intended, however, to be a rejection of ethical activity; rather, it is a way of accounting for the contribution of outsideness in self–other relations and the project of aesthetics. In an earlier essay, Bakhtin, 'Art and Answerability', in *Art and Answerability: Early Philosophical Essays by M.M. Bakhtin* (trans. Vadim Liapunov; supplement trans. Kenneth Brostrom; Austin, TX: University of Texas Press, 1990), 1-3 (1), argues that the three domains of human culture—science, art, and life—find unity of meaning only in the activity of the person who integrates them, which unity, Bakhtin insists, is the responsibility of human beings in daily life: 'I have to answer with my own life for what I have experienced and understood in art, so that everything I have experienced and understood would not remain ineffectual in my life.'

Although in this instance no information is provided regarding either the woman's understanding or her response to Jesus' loving glance, other examples reveal that the object of contemplation can itself experience a new birth within this loving glance. This, I propose, is what happens in many of the healing miracles: in response to the loving presence of Jesus there occurs a physical healing, a type of new birth (e.g. 8.1-4; 9.1-8, 18-26). In terms of Bakhtin's approach, this new birth represents a form of self-objectification on the part of the characters, which Bakhtin calls confessional self-accounting. Confessional self-accounting describes the condition wherein our inability to assemble the dispersed moments of our inner lives assumes a penitential tone and is in turn met by the authoritative, yet loving, glance of the beholder, who affirms in us what we rightly reject. Although the essential features of confessional self-accounting—the authoritative and the penitential—are not documented for each healing miracle, they are present often enough to support the contention that Bakhtin's definition of confessional self-accounting can be applied fruitfully to an examination of these character interactions in Matthew's Gospel.[32]

In the first place, Jesus is acknowledged by at least some of the other characters as having special authority: his teaching astonishes the crowds, who perceive that 'he taught them as one who had authority, and not as their scribes' (7.29). And when he heals the paralytic, the witnessing crowds 'glorified God, who had given such authority to men' (9.8). Finally, the risen Jesus himself declares to his disciples, 'All authority in heaven and on earth has been given to me' (28.18). Clearly, Matthew intends that Jesus be seen as the authoritative one.[33]

On the other hand, the necessary penitential tone is clearly evident in such examples as the healing of the two blind men, who cry out to Jesus, 'Have mercy on us, Son of David' (9.28). A more interesting expression of this penitential tone, however, can be imputed generally to those who have been excluded from the community of the people of Israel, such as those

---

32. The brief application of the principles of confessional self-accounting that follows is intended primarily to establish the theme of Jesus' unique role in the Gospel as an authoring hero. Other themes that are introduced in this will be developed more fully in the subsequent analyses of the Gospel's interactions between Jesus and the major character groups.

33. See Gundry, *Matthew*, 137-80, who develops the theme of Jesus' authority as demonstrated in his deeds (8.1-9.34), which complement his authoritative words (7.28-29).

with certain physical infirmities (e.g. leprosy) or those who associate with non-Jews (e.g. tax collectors). First, the very status of those who are excluded suggests that their tone is likely to be penitential (although it is certainly possible to harbor a defiant attitude in outcast isolation). More importantly, Jesus himself understands that his mission is to seek out those who have been excluded: when he is asked why he dines with tax collectors and sinners, Jesus replies, 'Those who are well have no need of a physician, but those who are sick' (9.12). And from the faith response of those whom Jesus heals, it seems apparent that they are aware of their sickness. In other words, a penitential tone is nothing more than the awareness of one's sickness, whether physical or metaphorical, and the inability to effect one's own healing. In terms of Bakhtin's 'what-is' and 'what-ought-to-be', no one can completely fulfill the 'ought' of the law; on the other hand, it is only those who have been excluded by the law who can truly understand the impossibility of its fulfillment: such as these have no hope for fulfilling their 'ought'. Yet, as Bakhtin argues, they are also unable to accept the condition of their 'is', they are unable to assemble all of their self-manifestations into a truly finalized whole of meaning. Thus they depend entirely on the loving other, the other who accepts their 'is' and makes possible a new birth.

As an 'author' in Matthew's Gospel, Jesus lovingly consummates the transgredient moments of other characters and makes possible their new birth. New birth is possible, however, only when the object of aesthetic contemplation acknowledges the authority of the beholder and meets the beholder's loving glance with a penitential tone. The failure of the Pharisees to respond to Jesus' aesthetic contemplation can therefore be attributed, from the perspective of Bakhtin's approach, either to their inability to acknowledge Jesus' authority or to the absence of a penitential tone. It appears that they fail on both counts.

One indication that the Pharisees are troubled by the source of Jesus' authority is evident in their claim that he casts out demons 'by Beelzebul, the prince of demons' (12.24). The chief priests and elders are similarly disturbed: they ask Jesus directly, 'By what authority are you doing these things, and who gave you this authority?' (21.23). Clearly, authority is not a self-claim, but an acknowledgment on the part of those who may have to overcome the limitation of their prior understanding. Thus the Pharisees (and the chief priests and elders), who apparently do not have eyes to see, cannot acknowledge Jesus' authority as an authority that is normative for them.

The reason for this inability to acknowledge Jesus' authority is quite possibly related to the absence of a penitential tone on their part: the Pharisees apparently believe (incorrectly) that they have no need of a penitential orientation, inasmuch as they are children of Abraham (3.8-9). By following the commandments, they have, in a certain sense, fulfilled their 'ought'. After all, according to Matthew, keeping the commandments is not impossible: the rich young man tells Jesus that he has observed all of the commandments (19.20). By keeping the commandments, the Pharisees are able to maintain their status within their community, a community that by definition would find it impossible to acknowledge the authority of one who eats with tax collectors and sinners, that is, one who breaks the law, at least as they understand it. For these reasons, the failure of the Pharisees to experience a new birth is not a failure of Jesus' loving glance, but the consequence of their inability, and perhaps their refusal, to acknowledge Jesus' authority and meet his loving glance with a penitential tone.

Reader–Character Interaction

This discussion of the unique role of Jesus as an authoring hero suggests an alternative to the reading strategy of Howell and others, which encourages the emulation of Jesus' ethical behavior. Inasmuch as Jesus is portrayed as an 'aestheticized' absolute consciousness, readers are precluded from approaching him directly by means of aesthetic contemplation: apart from those aspects of his characterization that are necessary for any type of character portrayal, the readers are unable to find a position that is entirely outside the consciousness of Jesus. The most significant limitation of Jesus' absolute knowledge—when the end will occur (24.36)—is unavailable to the readers as well. Another potential limitation—the knowledge that he is the Son of God (14.33; 16.16; 27.54)—is clearly the revelation of God (3.17; 16.17; 17.5), which is certainly not available to all the characters of the narrative (11.27), nor for that matter is it necessarily available, except conceptually, even to the readers of Matthew's Gospel. Without this stable position of outsideness with respect to Jesus, the readers cannot completely assemble the self-manifestations of Jesus into a unitary whole of meaning. Moreover, even the forward-directed inner life of Jesus, which the readers would be expected to co-experience in aesthetic contemplation, is not available to them in the same way that it is to Jesus: the encompassing nature of his consciousness places it on an entirely different level than the readers' own consciousness.

The interaction between Jesus and the other characters of Matthew's Gospel, on the other hand, does offer the readers an approach to Jesus—through the agency of the narrative's other characters, all of whom can be aesthetically contemplated. To approach Jesus through the other characters, however, is to reject characterization conceived primarily in terms of character traits, such as Kingsbury's description of Jesus as 'saving', 'authoritative', 'enabling', 'compassionate'.[34] Although these traits are correctly inferred from Jesus' interaction with the other characters, they are by definition characteristics abstracted from their narrative context. A more nuanced discussion of characterization is the one proposed by R. Alan Culpepper in his study of John's Gospel. Culpepper conceives characterization not as a static catalog of traits but a dynamic process of plot-focused character interactions: 'Instead of isolated units, the reader finds that the characters are profoundly related. They are in effect the prism which breaks up the pure light of Jesus' remote epiphany into colors the reader can see.'[35] Although Culpepper proceeds to interpret the characters' responses to Jesus as exemplifying desired reader outcomes, similar to the approach adopted by Howell, he correctly insists that the readers are able to come to knowledge of Jesus only by means of the characters' interaction with Jesus.

The reading strategy of this study, which posits Jesus as an 'aestheticized' absolute consciousness, similarly restricts the readers' access to Jesus: although, as often noted by literary critics, the readers in principle know more than the characters in the narrative world, they do not know more than the character Jesus of Nazareth. Therefore, the readers cannot approach Jesus in the same way that they do the other characters in Matthew's Gospel. Rather, in accordance with the methodology of this study, the readers must interact with the character Jesus by means of the other characters, who are themselves 'authored' by Jesus.

Categories of Relationship
The interactions between Jesus and the other characters of Matthew's Gospel, when approached from the perspective of aesthetic contemplation, can be described in terms of three categories of relationship, which Bakhtin uses throughout his essay 'Author and Hero in Aesthetic Activity'. These categories express either the forward-directedness of life experi-

34. Kingsbury, *Matthew as Story*, 13.
35. R. Alan Culpepper, *Anatomy of the Fourth Gospel: A Study in Literary Design* (Philadelphia: Fortress Press, 1983), 104.

enced from within the hero or the finalizing images produced by an author who assembles the hero's self-manifestations into a unitary whole of meaning: (1) the category *I-for-myself* refers to how I, the hero, look to my own consciousness; (2) the category *I-for-others* refers to how I look to others, who assemble finalizing images of me; and (3) the category *others-for-me* refers to how others look to me, a category that reverses the role of authorship. Inasmuch as the primary role of Jesus, as posited in this study, is the role of authoring hero, then the place of 'other' in these categories of relationship is filled by Jesus. The categories of otherness could therefore be redefined as (1) *I-for-Jesus*, or how a character appears to Jesus; and (2) *Jesus-for-me*, or how Jesus appears to a character.

These categories of relationship establish a framework for analyzing the interactions between Jesus and the Gospel's major character groups—the Pharisees, the disciples and the supplicants. The role of the readers, which Bakhtin understands as a type of secondary authoring, is to encounter Jesus of Nazareth through his interactions with these other characters. These interactions place the readers in the position of holding together the limited perspective of the narrative's characters and the fuller perspective of the narrative's surplus, which the readers share with the author of Matthew's Gospel. The expected outcome of this reading strategy is that the readers, who confess Jesus of Nazareth to be the risen Lord, will also be forced to co-experience the limited perspective of the narrative's major character groups, each of which are confronted by the veil of Jesus' ordinariness. The explanation of the varied responses of the character groups—rejection, unfruitful reception and fruitful reception—is to be found in the characters' interactions with Jesus. However, the readers' activity of co-authoring these character interactions, as the activity is conceptualized by this study, is not intended so much to discover an explanation for the characters' responses as it is to present the readers with the one who is able to reconstitute an unredeemed heart. This encounter is possible because the readers not only co-experience the limited perspective of the narrative's characters but they do so in a way that the characters themselves cannot: inasmuch as the readers also co-author the interactions between Jesus and the other characters, they have knowledge that is in principle unavailable to the characters. Subsequently, in accordance with Bakhtin's project, the readers must answer with their own lives for what they have learned in their encounter with Jesus of Nazareth, for what they have experienced and understood in the art of Matthew's Gospel.

Chapter 4

THE DISCIPLES

Reader–Disciple Role Identity

After Jesus the most important character in Matthew's Gospel is the character group the disciples. Unlike Jesus, however, their importance does not lie so much in their role as plot functionaries—as Kingsbury notes, '[e]xcept for Judas's act of betrayal and perhaps the climactic resurrection scene in Galilee (28.16-20), the disciples do not greatly influence the plot, or flow, of Matthew's story'[1]—but in their role as the primary recipients of Jesus' teaching. In this capacity the disciples are, of all the major characters in Matthew's Gospel, the ones who exhibit the most favorable response toward Jesus (13.51; 16.12). On the other hand, it is also true that there are significant negative aspects to the disciples' characterization as well, both of faith (8.26; 14.31; 17.20; 28.17) and understanding (15.16; 16.9; 16.23), implying a failure on the part of the disciples to embody completely the teaching of Jesus. Although it is conceivable that this mixed portrayal of the disciples represents a historically accurate account of the disciples' part in the public ministry of Jesus, the assertion is not only impossible to prove, but also, in light of the postmodern challenge to the notion of objective reporting, an unlikely construal of the evidence.[2] Even the redaction-critical explanation of the disciples' inconsistency as reflective of the mixed state of Matthew's community is weakened by the same inability to demonstrate the historicity of the reconstructions of redaction critics. Regardless of one's position on the matter of historicity, however, there remains the task

---

1. Kingsbury, *Matthew as Story*, 13.
2. See, for example, Via, *Revelation*, 100-103, who argues that the Gospel narratives disclose the familiar world and traditions about Jesus in a new light by de-familiarizing them. Although Via speaks about Gospel narratives in particular, he implies that all narratives, inasmuch as they are fundamentally imaginative compositions, perform the same function.

of describing the readers' interaction with the disciples as they are portrayed in the narrative itself.

Despite using different methodologies, Matthean scholars have tended to agree that the character group the disciples functions for the readers as the narrative's principal link to Jesus' teaching. For the most part this conclusion relies upon the generally unstated presupposition that the readers of Matthew's Gospel are themselves disciples of Jesus: inasmuch as the readers share the same role as the disciples, they are encouraged to identify with their narrative counterparts, especially with respect to the disciples' role as the principal recipients of Jesus' teaching.[3] Scholars have tended to disagree, on the other hand, about the extent of the readers' identification with the disciples.

Matthew's Example of Imperfect Followers

Redaction critics, those who tend to perceive a strong correlation between the Gospel's character groups and Matthew's historical community, have proposed alternative approaches for understanding Matthew's characterization of the disciples. For some scholars, 'disciples' is a technical term referring to the Twelve—whether historical figures or historicized figures who are part of 'a unique, unrepeatable, holy, and ideal epoch in the course of history'.[4] For others, the disciples serve as a transparency onto Matthew's community, whether the community itself[5] or its leaders.[6] Michael Wilkins, on the other hand, has argued that these approaches tend to

3. Paul E. Jose and William F. Brewer, 'Development of Story Liking: Character Identification, Suspense and Outcome Resolution', *Developmental Psychology* 20 (1984), 911-24, have shown that empathic identification, in which the reader steps into the character's role, is a phenomenon attested in readers by the time they reach the sixth grade. In another study Paul E. Jose, 'The Role of Gender and Gender Role Similarity in Readers' Identification with Story Characters', *Sex Roles* 21 (1989), 697-713, defended the hypothesis that adult subjects are more likely to identify with characters when they perceive gender role similarities between themselves and the characters than when there is simply gender correspondence.

4. Georg Strecker, 'The Concept of History in Matthew', in Graham Stanton (ed.), *The Interpretation of Matthew* (London: SPCK, 1983), 73. See also William Foxwell Albright and C. S. Mann, *Matthew* (AB, 26; Garden City, NY: Doubleday, 1971), lxxvii.

5. For example, Ulrich Luz, 'The Disciples in the Gospel According to Matthew', in Graham Stanton (ed.), *The Interpretation of Matthew* (London: SPCK, 1983), 98-128.

6. For example, Minear, *Matthew*, 10-11.

overlap, precluding the need to choose one over the other.[7] Wilkins, following John J. Vincent,[8] proposes instead that Matthew's portrait of the disciples serves both purposes—it passes on the historical tradition of the Twelve and presents them as examples of discipleship to his community.

According to Wilkins's model, Matthew has selected traditional material about the disciples that meets the needs of his community, rather than reading his own situation into his historical traditions. Wilkins argues that by portraying the disciples 'as they really were', a portrayal that includes both positive and negative responses, Matthew sets forth 'an example of what his church should be'.[9] According to Wilkins, the occasions when the disciples are characterized positively show the readers 'what will happen to true disciples who fully obey and follow Jesus (especially presented in the discipleship teachings)'.[10]   On the other hand, when the disciples fail to embody fully the teaching of Jesus, this negative characterization shows Matthew's readers what can happen to disciples 'who do not identify with Jesus in his obedience to the will of the Father'.[11] In both instances, the responses of the disciples are evaluated and consequences determined on the basis of their adherence to the teaching of Jesus. Thus, the mixed portrayal of the disciples is said to provide Matthew's readers with a positive example of encouragement, a negative example of warning, but especially it provides them with the example of imperfect followers 'who are able to overcome their lackings through the teaching of Jesus'.[12]

Wilkins's proposal to settle the debate of whether to view the disciples as historical figures or character transparencies of the community, for the most part incorporates both approaches. Although he clearly favors the view that the disciples are historical figures, they are historical figures who have been made relevant for the church as 'examples of what Jesus, with his people, can accomplish'.[13] Inasmuch as the evangelist is believed to

7.   Michael J. Wilkins, *The Concept of Disciple in Matthew's Gospel as Reflected in the Use of the Term* Mathētēs (Leiden: E.J. Brill, 1988), 168-69. See also Robert A. Guelich, *The Sermon on the Mount: A Foundation for Understanding* (Waco, TX: Word Books, 1982), 53; Benno Przybylski, *Righteousness in Matthew and his World of Thought* (SNTMS, 41; Cambridge: Cambridge University Press, 1980), 109.

8.   John James Vincent, 'Discipleship and Synoptic Studies', *TZ* 16 (1960), 456-569 (464).

9.   Wilkins, *Concept of Disciple*, 169.

10.   Wilkins, *Concept of Disciple*, 169.

11.   Wilkins, *Concept of Disciple*, 169.

12.   Wilkins, *Concept of Disciple*, 222.

13.   Wilkins, *Concept of Disciple*, 224.

have selected certain historical traditions that address the needs of his community, it can be argued that the portrayal of the disciples also reflects the community's situation. Although Wilkins's analysis does not examine the implications of his position for defining the composition of Matthew's readers, it is implied that the evangelist's community consists of imperfect followers for whom the adherence to Jesus' teaching is essential.

By describing the role of the character group the disciples as the readers' example of positive and negative behavior, Wilkins offers a convincing explanation of the disciples' role, not only for Matthew's historical readers, but for subsequent generations of readers as well. In the case of Matthew's historical audience the possibility that some readers would have recognized themselves in the narrative only enhances the cogency of Wilkins's model. The challenge of Wilkins's model, however, is to explain the mechanism of reader–character interaction for subsequent readers, an investigation that clearly belongs to the purview of literary critics. But even the interaction between Matthew's historical readers and the character group the disciples, inasmuch as it is predicated on the reception of a literary paradigm, also requires the analysis of literary critics. This is because, arguably, all readers must be able to see Jesus and hear his words in the same way that the disciples do in order for the disciples to function truly as examples for the readers. In other words, the readers must co-experience, at least in some form, the disciples' limited perspective, expressed as the literary configuration that represents the character group, in order to be able to actualize the discipleship pattern of Matthew's Gospel.[14]

Schooling the Reader in Discipleship Values

The narrative critic David Howell has also argued that the disciples, in their role as Jesus' narrative audience, function for the readers as the principal link to Jesus' teaching.[15] Howell has been critical, however, of interpretations that emphasize the perception of role identity as the primary means of including readers in the story world of Matthew's Gospel.[16] While acknowledging that a combination of role identity and positive characterization has indeed encouraged actual readers to identify with the

---

14. This approach recalls the suggestion of Wayne A. Meeks, 'A Hermeneutics of Social Embodiment', *HTR* 79 (1986), 176-86 (184), that regardless of one's opinion of a text, its full understanding requires 'a participation at least in the imagination, an empathy with the kind of communal life which "fits" the text'.

15. Howell, *Matthew's Inclusive Story*, 246.

16. Howell, *Matthew's Inclusive Story*, 229-30.

disciples, Howell nevertheless argues that the intended response to the Gospel's discipleship demands is embodied in the implied reader construct, not in the character group the disciples. This is primarily because the implied reader occupies a position superior to the character group the disciples, which enables the readers to have access to information that is not available to the disciples, such as the Gospel's introductory material and the narrator's commentary. The readers' simple identification with the character group the disciples, on the other hand, would not only exclude aspects of the Gospel's narrative rhetoric, it would, according to Howell, inappropriately restrict the readers' involvement in the Gospel's narrative world: 'If the implied reader is identified with the character group the disciples, only those values and attitudes which are displayed by the disciples in the plotted story become exemplary for the actual readers.'[17] This means that the positive characterization of non-disciples, such as Joseph (1.19, 24), the Roman centurion (8.10), and the Canaanite woman (15.28), would not be a part of the narrative rhetoric that is intended to influence actual readers. The negative traits of the disciples, on the other hand, would be included, which traits clearly do not represent the values of the implied author. In other words, if identification is viewed primarily as the readers' acceptance of the character's values and emulation of the character's behavior, then the disciples' conflicting character traits represent a potential problem for actual readers.

On the other hand, by defining discipleship as the proper response to Jesus, which is actualized as the implied reader construct rather than as membership in the character group the disciples, actual readers are encouraged to identify with the characters or distance themselves from them, depending on how the Gospel's rhetoric grants or withholds approval. The consequence of such granting or withholding of approval, as Kingsbury explains, is 'that the reader becomes schooled in the values that govern the life of discipleship in Matthew's story'.[18] For example, the initial, positive response of the disciples to Jesus' call (4.18-22) establishes the disciples in the subsequent scene (chs. 5–7) as the exemplary recipients of Jesus' teaching: 'Jesus invites people to follow him, and his teaching is directed to those who, like the disciples, are obedient to his interpretation of God's will.'[19] When the disciples fail to embody consistently the teaching of

---

17. Howell, *Matthew's Inclusive Story*, 233.
18. Kingsbury, *Matthew as Story*, 14.
19. Howell, *Matthew's Inclusive Story*, 246.

Jesus, the readers are encouraged on those occasions, not only to judge the disciples negatively, but to look to Jesus for the model of obedience.

Howell's criticism of the transparency concept, which is posited on the readers' expected identification with the character group the disciples, is not without merit. As Howell correctly insists, the narrative's rhetorical effects are not limited to those effects that the readers encounter simply by identifying with the disciples: 'The disciples neither embody all the values and norms commended by the implied author, nor do they know everything about Jesus which would help the Matthean church members and other actual readers respond properly to Jesus.'[20] Upon closer examination, however, several important criticisms of Howell's approach become evident. In the first place, this solution does not address the function of the disciples' mixed characterization for readers who already approve of the Gospel's values. In other words, it is not clear how the narrative functions in the case of readers who not only know the story's outcome, but also claim to endorse its values. Redaction critics, on the other hand, would argue that the Gospel was addressed in particular to those members of Matthew's community who were living without reference to the Gospel's values, reminding them of their prior confession. Second, inasmuch as these same values are assigned to other characters, whether as the positive characterization of the supplicants or the negative characterization of the Pharisees, the reason for presenting the disciples with conflicting traits becomes less clear. Again, redaction critics would argue that the Gospel's mixed portrayal of the disciples represents the characterization of the members of Matthew's historical community, for whom the perception of role identity would have been the primary means of confronting them with their discipleship shortcomings. Finally, inasmuch as the implied reader, indeed every reader, occupies a position of greater knowledge with respect to the narrative's characters, the characterization of the disciples as the principal recipients of the teaching of Jesus, although an accurate description of the disciples' narrative role, does not seem to be an adequate description of their role for the readers.

The Readers as Imperfect Followers

Because, for Howell, the concept of identification implies the acceptance of the characters' values, he limits its application to the readers' identification with positive characters, or, in the case of mixed characters, such as

20. Howell, *Matthew's Inclusive Story*, 235.

the disciples, to those occasions when the characters respond positively. Consequently, positive characterizations, inasmuch as they represent the desired reader outcome, essentially establish Howell's definition of the reader, or at least the reader's expected predisposition. For example, Howell interprets the disciples' initial, obedient response to the call of Jesus as indicative of 'the kind of audience for which such teaching may be appropriate'.[21] Overlooked by Howell is the possibility that negative characterizations would serve a similar purpose, by defining the kind of audience that needs to hear Jesus' teaching, not unlike the description of the mixed, historical community that is frequently proposed by redaction critics. In other words, when the readers of Matthew's Gospel apprehend the mixed portrayal of the disciples on the basis of role identity, the portrayal does not merely imply discipleship shortcomings on the part of Matthew's historical readers or suggest the possibility of discipleship shortcomings in general, it actually addresses all readers of Matthew's Gospel as imperfect disciples *in fact*.

The most important implication of this proposal is that unless the readers understand that they too are imperfect disciples, then the Gospel, although addressed to them, will not be welcomed by them as the good news that is able to reconstitute their heart, the seat of their understanding and intention, which, as I argue, is a defensible explanation of the function of Matthew's Gospel, whether or not it represents the evangelist's own intention.[22] This line of reasoning suggests the importance of answering the question, Why don't the disciples fully embody the teaching of Jesus? The question does not apparently occur to Howell, however, possibly because his use of the implied reader construct tends to focus his attention primarily on the readers' appropriation of the evangelist's values. But if one accepts the proposal that the mixed characterization of the disciples serves to define the readers themselves as imperfect followers, primarily by making use of their perception of role equivalence, then the problem of the disciples' failure to actualize Jesus' teaching becomes in principle the

---

21. Howell, *Matthew's Inclusive Story*, 246.

22. Garland, *Reading Matthew*, 4-7, conveniently summarizes the leading proposals of the purpose of Matthew's Gospel: (1) to tell the story of Jesus; (2) to bolster faith; (3) to convince and refute; (4) to explain present circumstances; (5) to exhort; and (6) to arm for mission. When Garland subsequently asks why the discourse of ch. 23 should be addressed specifically to the disciples, and not to the scribes and Pharisees, he concludes that it serves as a type of exhortation, a warning to the church 'that they had better not be found false stewards like the scribes and Pharisees' (229).

readers' problem as well, a problem ultimately of the readers' own self-understanding. Only a methodology that does not reject out of hand the negative character traits that are encountered during the process of the readers' interaction with the character group the disciples permits the readers to be defined by these traits as well. The presupposition of Howell's literary-critical approach, on the other hand, is that negative responses function as examples of the types of behavior that are to be avoided.

Aesthetic Contemplation

Howell's appropriation of the implied reader as a construct that selectively values character traits, preferring positive traits over negative ones, resembles Bakhtin's description of the way we human beings in life react to the self-manifestations of others: we respond not to the whole of an individual but to those parts of an individual's activity that are of special interest to us. Even our attempts to consider the whole of an individual do not represent an encompassing definition, but 'a prognosis of what we can and what we cannot expect from him'.[23] Bakhtin's analysis of aesthetic activity demonstrates that it is only the author of an aesthetic work who is able to overcome the volitional orientation of everyday life by assembling all of the hero's self-manifestations into a whole of meaning. When the readers, in Bakhtin's sense, co-author the aesthetic work, they, like the author, accept all of the hero's self-manifestations, whether good or evil, and assemble them into a finalized whole of meaning, thereby transposing that life onto the aesthetic plane. In the case of Matthew's Gospel, this means that the readers momentarily accept the limitation of the disciples' horizon or perspective, subsequently placing it in the context of the narrative's finalizing environment, in order to be addressed in the same way that the character group the disciples is addressed—by the authoring activity of Jesus of Nazareth.

The Disciples' Unfinalizable Task

The disciples' self-manifestations—their words and deeds—represent the expression of their forward-directed inner life, which they are unable from within themselves to assemble into a finalized whole of meaning. The reason is that the disciples lack the perspective from which to encompass the entirety of their life, that is, they lack the finalizing, axiological

---

23. Bakhtin, 'Author and Hero', 5.

vantage point afforded by death. Unless this perspective is achieved, however, every action, whether ethical or cognitive, is by definition devoid of ultimate meaning 'in the way a task is hostile to not-being-fulfilled-yet, or what-ought-to-be is hostile to what-is, or atonement is hostile to sin'.[24] Insofar as the disciples function as the narrative recipients of Jesus' teaching, they are by definition characters who are continually confronted with a task—the task of obeying all of the commandments of Jesus, a task that is implied in the Gospel's concluding pericope: 'Go therefore and make disciples of all nations, baptizing them in the name of the Father and of the Son and of the Holy Spirit, teaching them to observe all that I have commanded you' (28.19-20). Consequently, the disciples' failure to embody fully the teaching of Jesus can be understood as an expression of the tension between what-ought-to-be and what-is, in Bakhtin's sense.

This interpretation is supported by the so-called antitheses of the sermon on the mount (5.21-48), which are frequently interpreted to be an intensification of the law. The final commandment of Jesus in this series—'You, therefore, must be perfect, as your heavenly Father is perfect' (5.48)—arguably expresses the impossibility of ever completing one's responsibility,[25] even if Matthew himself may have believed that the commandments of Jesus could be accomplished. Further underscoring the nature of the commandments as an unfinalizable task are the judgment pericopes, which occur near the end of each of the discourses. These pericopes, especially the parable of the last judgment (25.31-46), disclose the post-mortem perspective that will eventually confront and finalize each of the disciples. Therefore, the inability of the disciples to accomplish the commandments fully is, in a sense, the expression of the open-endedness of a life that is perceived from within. But it is also more than that.

An important consequence of the disciples' inability to assemble the dispersed moments of their forward-directed inner life is that they, like human beings in life, are driven instead to seek the consummated images of themselves in the authoring activity of others. Although even these images can never actually consummate the disciples, inasmuch as they are always surmounted by the disciples' own consciousness, it is possible that the authoring activity of others would evoke on the part of the disciples the response of confessional self-accounting, the act of potential self-determination consequent to ethical reflection. Inasmuch as it is ultimately the

24. Bakhtin, 'Author and Hero', 122.

25. Even though the rich young man had kept all of the commandments, his refusal to follow Jesus (19.16-22) suggests a similar inability to accomplish the law fully.

readers' responsibility, standing in the place of the author of the aesthetic event, to co-author the disciples' dispersed inner life, this suggests that the failure of the disciples to embody completely the teaching of Jesus also creates the possibility of an act of confessional self-accounting on the part of the readers, who are confronted by the same unfinalizable task. The purpose of the readers' interaction with the disciples, however, as defined by the approach of aesthetic contemplation, is not for the readers to respond directly to Jesus and his teaching; rather, the purpose is to experience the limited perspective of the disciples in a different key than they themselves are able to do. In other words, the purpose of the readers' interaction with the character group the disciples, which is a co-experiencing of the disciples' inner life against the background of their transgredient moments, is to discover the reason for the disciples' failure by experiencing their perspective—as a linguistic structure—in the category of the other.

The first step of aesthetic contemplation is for the readers to project themselves into the disciples, assimilating the linguistic structure of their words and deeds as expressed in their character interactions, in order to be able to see the world as the disciples see it with all of its limitations with respect to time, space, value and meaning. The readers' identification with the disciples' limited perspective corresponds to a remarkable extent to the sequential-temporal aspect of reading, as it is often characterized by narrative and reader-response critics. There are, however, two important differences. The first difference is that the narrator's commentary, which is available to the implied reader sequentially as the narrative unfolds but not to the characters themselves, is bracketed by the readers of aesthetic contemplation during the moment of co-experiencing the hero's limited perspective. The second difference is that the entire narrative, including events and commentary that only become available to the implied reader sequentially, is available to the readers at whatever time they utilize their outsideness with respect to both the hero and the narrative for the purpose of consummating the hero's transgredient moments. It is by reassuming their position of surplus with respect to the characters that the readers are able to experience the characters' limited perspective in a different key.

The readers of aesthetic contemplation co-experience the inner life of the disciples by assimilating the disciples' self-manifestations, that is, their words, deeds, thoughts and intentions. Narrative critics, on the other hand, generally use a character's self-manifestations to infer the character's traits, a process of accumulation that resembles Bakhtin's description of most attempts in life to provide an encompassing definition of a person, which definition is in fact merely a prognosis of what one can or cannot expect from that person. Nevertheless, a narrative-critical analysis of characteriztion, insofar as it relies on a sequential-temporal model of reading, represents a useful starting point for describing a character's limited perspective.

Character-Shaping Incidents

Richard Edwards, in his narrative-critical study of Matthew's disciples, cautions against understanding characterization simply as the accumulation of various traits over the course of a narrative.[26] He correctly insists that inasmuch as the disciples are present in many different scenes, the interpretation of the disciples' activity presupposes a careful examination of the specific incidents and their respective contexts according to the narrative sequence. On the other hand, simply to combine the traits, a procedure that ultimately renders both the incidents and their contexts irrelevant, is at best, according to Edwards, 'appropriate within redaction criticism, assuming that the author/editor has a consistent point of view throughout the story'.[27] Such an approach has the effect of privileging the evangelist's theology behind the text, rather than attending to the narrative itself. Edwards's narrative-critical study of the disciples, on the other hand, focuses on the role of the narrative as it forms the readers' understanding of the disciples.

Edwards's criticism of the practice of accumulating traits does not, however, represent a rejection of trait-focused approaches to characterization. Indeed, Edwards himself defines characterization as 'the techniques used in the narrative which guide the [text-connoted reader] to attach specific traits or attributes to the characters'.[28] Rather, he insists that a trait must always be related to the specific incident that gives rise to it. Contradictory traits, therefore, represent a variance at a particular moment in the story, which may be resolved later in the story when the text-connoted reader receives more information, but which must not be resolved simply by rejecting one trait and accepting another. Therefore, as long as one recognizes that context and sequence are necessarily constitutive of characterization, then the analysis of characterization becomes primarily a process of inferring traits from specific narrative indicators.

26.   Richard A. Edwards, *Matthew's Narrative Portrait of Disciples: How the Text-Connoted Reader Is Informed* (Harrisburg, PA: Trinity Press International, 1997), 11.
27.   Edwards, *Portrait of Disciples*, 11.
28.   Edwards, *Portrait of Disciples*, 11. The text-connoted reader is Edwards's version of the implied reader.

Edwards has identified five narrative features that enable the text-connoted reader to recognize the traits of an individual or group character: (1) the actions of a character; (2) the words of a character; (3) the narrator's description of a character, especially when it provides information about the character's internal response to some event; (4) the reaction of other characters; and (5) the expectation expressed by other characters.[29] Edwards's comments concerning these narrative features suggest the importance he ascribes to character traits as indicators of a character's inner life, which underscores the usefulness of his scheme for the project of aesthetic contemplation. For example, when the narrator simply reports an action, this is said to be a limited form of characterization: without additional information 'it is not very clear about the rationale for such an action'.[30] The same is true of speech. On the other hand, when the narrator describes a character's internal response to an event, such as the narrator's report that 'the men marveled' at the calming of the storm (8.27), this is considered to be 'more revealing'.[31] As Edwards observes, however, Matthew's Gospel 'is told in small action/speech units which contain little explanation from the narrator about the circumstances surrounding the incident or about the thoughts of the characters'.[32] Consequently, the motivation of the disciples' self-manifestations must be inferred from their speech and action, especially when they interact with other characters. Character interaction, therefore, provides 'the most important and informative data for a study of the characterization of the disciples'.[33]

By emphasizing the disciples' interaction with other characters Edwards essentially establishes the criterion for selecting the incidents that are primarily responsible for influencing the readers' understanding of the disciples, which Edwards calls character-shaping incidents. Character-shaping incidents 'are fundamentally those that contain a definite response by a disciple or the disciple group to an action or saying'.[34] Inasmuch as Jesus is the Gospel's most important character, the response of the disciples to his words and deeds 'reveals more about them than any other statement'.[35] Although the disciples' response may constitute the methodology's princi-

---

29. Edwards, *Portrait of Disciples*, 12-13.
30. Edwards, *Portrait of Disciples*, 12.
31. Edwards, *Portrait of Disciples*, 12.
32. Edwards, *Portrait of Disciples*, 13.
33. Edwards, *Portrait of Disciples*, 13.
34. Edwards, *Portrait of Disciples*, 15.
35. Edwards, *Portrait of Disciples*, 15.

pal criterion, incidents that do not report a response are nevertheless important for establishing the necessary context of subsequent events.

Jesus and the Disciples

Inasmuch as the forward-directedness of a hero's inner life, which the readers seek to co-experience, resembles to a considerable extent the sequential-temporal aspect of reading, Edwards's approach represents a useful method for establishing the limited horizon of the character group the disciples. However, unlike the sequential-temporal reader typical of narrative and reader-response criticism, the reader of aesthetic contemplation is defined as a construct that momentarily accepts the limitations of a character's horizon in order subsequently to fill in those limitations with the character's transgredient moments. In other words, Edwards's reader is most useful for establishing the limitations of the disciples' inner life; the reader of aesthetic contemplation, on the other hand, not only for the most part accepts the sequential-temporal limitations of Edwards's approach, but also accounts for the consummating perspective that belongs to the author of the aesthetic work and is shared by the readers.

Although Edwards has identified 11 character-shaping incidents involving the disciples, two of them—the Call of Peter, Andrews, James and John (Mt. 4.18-22) and the Stilling of the Storm (Mt. 8.23-27)—present a special challenge for the reader of aesthetic contemplation, inasmuch as at this stage in the narrative the disciples do not understand the nature of Jesus' authority (8.27), but the readers do understand (1.21; 3.16; 28.18). Nevertheless, Jesus scolds the disciples for their little faith (8.26). Jesus' characterization of the disciples as those of little faith, a characterization that would otherwise represent a limited reaction to part of the disciples' activity, is in fact, according to the methodology of this study, an encompassing definition of the disciples: not only does Jesus, as the narrative's unique authoring hero, subsequently repeat the characterization of the disciples in different contexts (14.31; 17.20), but the narrator also confirms Jesus' encompassing words, reporting in the Gospel's final scene that the disciples doubted when they assembled before the risen Lord (28.17).

Matthew 4.18-22
The first character-shaping incident involving the disciples is Matthew's account of the call of Peter, Andrew, James and John. Edwards classifies the pericope as a character-shaping incident because it not only depicts the

disciples' response to the command of Jesus to follow him, it also provides 'an indication of Jesus' understanding of his purpose and goals'.[36] The response takes the form of an action, for which the narrator offers no explanation, leaving scholars to infer from the context the value of the response, and in some cases, its rationale as well.

The most common interpretation considers the disciples' response to be positive. Inasmuch as the disciples immediately leave their occupation and their family to follow Jesus,[37] their response appears to represent an acknowledgment of Jesus' authority.[38] This interpretation is subsequently confirmed by the incident of the reluctant disciple who seeks permission first to bury his father: Jesus insists on the priority of his call (8.21-22). Similarly, when Peter reminds Jesus after his encounter with the rich man that they have left everything to follow him, Jesus acknowledges the positive value of their response, assuring them that they will receive their future reward (19.27-29). This standard explanation of the call of the disciples, however, is suitable only in the case of the sequential-temporal reader, for whom the narrator has established Jesus' authority in the preceding narrative, not for the disciples themselves.[39] Despite Edwards's suggestion that the disciples may have heard the preaching of Jesus and repented,[40] it is unclear that the authority of Jesus is in fact a consideration for the disciples.

An alternative, although not entirely unrelated, explanation, which better approximates the disciples' limited horizon, is based on the interpretation of Jesus' words—'I will make you fishers of men'—as a promise having 'great appeal to these men'.[41] Although most scholars interpret

---

36. Edwards, *Portrait of Disciples*, 20.

37. See Craig S. Keener, *A Commentary on the Gospel of Matthew* (Grand Rapids: Eerdmans, 1999), 151-55, for a discussion of the possible economic and social costs of Jesus' call.

38. Patte, *Matthew*, 57, contends that, whatever may have been the disciples' motivation for obeying, 'Jesus' authority is manifested in such a way that they cannot but obey him'.

39. See Warren Carter, 'Matthew 4.18-22 and Matthean Discipleship: An Audience-Oriented Perspective', *CBQ* 59 (1997), 58-75 (62-65).

40. Edwards, *Portrait of Disciples*, 26.

41. Edwards, *Portrait of Disciples*, 22, proposes that inasmuch as the brothers are fishermen they would respond positively to the invitation to fish for people. Although authority is not explicitly made an issue here, it is implied that Jesus is able to accomplish what he promises. While Edwards's suggestion establishes a metaphorical connection between the disciples' current and future professions, it does not actually

'fishers of men' as a reference to Jer. 16.16-18,[42] there is no evidence that the disciples understand the allusion. Therefore, a more likely explanation, especially in light of the disciples' subsequent misunderstanding of Jesus' mission (e.g. 16.21-24), is that they perceive these words as a promise of a new status that will bring them authority and power: as the reader of aesthetic contemplation already knows, the disciples are subsequently given authority over unclean spirits and diseases (10.1), promised the keys of the kingdom (16.19) and thrones of judgment (19.28), but they are also rebuked for seeking places of honor in the kingdom (20.20-28). According to this interpretation, the willingness of the disciples to change is a positive element of their characterization. On the other hand, the disciples' likely expectation of improved status, which knowledge is available to the reader of aesthetic contemplation, introduces a negative element into their characterization as well.

Matthew 8.23-27

The stilling of the storm adds to the readers' understanding of the disciples, primarily by depicting their response to Jesus against the expectations of the story's context, which includes in particular Jesus' teaching (5–7) and his appraisal of the centurion's faith (8.5-13). Unlike the initial character-shaping incident, which he considers to be a positive portrayal of the disciples despite lacking an adequate context to establish motivation and expectation, Edwards interprets the storm pericope as presenting a mixed image of the disciples. When the disciples realize that the storm is about to swamp their boat, they awaken Jesus, imploring him to save them. Edwards interprets the disciples' actions as indicative of their fear, but also of their belief that Jesus 'can do something to protect them'.[43] In view of the circumstances, the actions of the disciples are understandable; it is the reaction of Jesus, on the other hand, who questions their fear, referring to them as 'men of little faith' (8.26), that appears to be unreasonable. When Jesus subsequently calms the storm, it provokes the disciples to wonder what sort of man he is, implying that the disciples do not understand the nature of Jesus' authority, despite what they have previously heard and witnessed. Nevertheless, the inability of the disciples to recognize Jesus' authority is not unexpected: according to Edwards, the teaching

---

explain why the promise should be appealing. He observes that the metaphor itself remains a gap that the text-connoted reader must subsequently fill in.

42. E.g. Davies and Allison, *Matthew*, I, 398; Gundry, *Matthew*, 62.

43. Edwards, *Portrait of Disciples*, 30.

of Jesus, which forms the main context of this story, itself establishes that the disciples 'are likely to perform at a low level and can be expected to fall short of his expectation'.[44] The disciples' request for help confirms that they are indeed 'men of little faith'.

The readers, on the other hand, who have knowledge of the narrator's commentary and the events prior to the call of the disciples (Mt. 1–4), understand the christological aspect of this narrative. Therefore, Davies and Allison conclude that 'for the implied readers the meaning of 8.23-27 cannot be the disciples' query'.[45] Rather, the readers' question must be, 'Do they trust their Lord in the storms of life, or are they, despite the revelation made known to them, of little faith?'[46] Their conclusion follows Bornkamm's interpretation that the story is 'a kerygmatic paradigm of the danger and glory of discipleship'.[47]

The interpretation of Davies and Allison accounts for the readers' involvement in the narrative by shifting the story's emphasis from the disciples' concluding exclamation to their request that Jesus should save them. Davies and Allison support their analysis with compositional evidence, arguing that the pericope is chiastically structured, its center coinciding with the disciples' plea to Jesus.[48] Gundry, on the other hand, while recognizing that the story begins with a stress on discipleship, argues that it ultimately becomes a tale of Jesus' majesty.[49] Gundry bases his interpretation in part on the unexpected use of *seismos*, a word otherwise associated with eschatological events in Matthew's Gospel: the birth-pangs before the end (24.7), Jesus' crucifixion (27.54) and his resurrection (28.2). He concludes that Jesus' rebuke of the disciples on account of their little faith 'implies that the disciples should have seen in the great shaking a sign of his majesty rather than a threat'.[50] Gundry's interpretation, however, does not explain why the disciples should have recognized the storm as a sign of majesty, since this is the first occurrence of *seismos* in Matthew's Gospel. By the time the sea has been calmed, which is itself evidence of Jesus' authority, the disciples are no longer in the same position with respect to knowledge as they were prior to the storm. Rather, it is only the

---

44. Edwards, *Portrait of Disciples*, 38.
45. Davies and Allison, *Matthew*, II, 70.
46. Davies and Allison, *Matthew*, II, 70.
47. Bornkamm, 'Stilling of the Storm', 57.
48. Davies and Allison, *Matthew*, II, 68.
49. Gundry, *Matthew*, 155.
50. Gundry, *Matthew*, 156.

reader of aesthetic contemplation who is aware of the storm's christological implications, as defined by Gundry, on the basis of events that are
beyond the limits of the disciples' awareness. Nevertheless, Gundry's conclusion essentially confirms that of Davies and Allison with respect to the
limited perspective of the disciples: despite what the disciples have been
taught and what they have witnessed, they do not understand the nature of
Jesus' authority.

Davies and Allison, Gundry and Edwards all agree that Jesus' rebuke of
the disciples indicates that he expected them to recognize his authority,
their fear expressing instead the anxious self-concern that Jesus had previously warned against (6.24-34).[51] Yet if this story is to be understood as 'a
call not to come to faith but rather to exercise the faith one already has',[52]
then the disciples are severely disadvantaged, inasmuch as they lack the
readers' finalizing perspective. The storm and Jesus' rebuke do not confront the readers in the same way that they do the disciples, unless the
readers are able momentarily to co-experience the disciples' limited horizon. Certainly, it is possible to recognize progress in the sequential-temporal reader's understanding of discipleship as something 'more than just
someone obeying Jesus or following him closely as he moves around
Galilee'.[53] But it is also true that progress in the disciples' understanding
of Jesus and the nature of his authority is more difficult to measure: as
Edwards demonstrates in his analysis of the remaining character-shaping
incidents, the disciples continue to be characterized as limited followers.
Indeed, although they are ultimately commissioned to preach the gospel to
all nations (28.19-20), it is only after they have once again exhibited the
limitedness of their discipleship: when they meet the risen Lord on the
mountain, 'they worshiped him; but some doubted' (28.17).

The Ongoing Challenge of Those Who Are with Jesus
Inasmuch as the mixed portrayal of the disciples appears to be related to
their failure to grasp fully the nature of Jesus' authority, the question then
becomes, Why doesn't the authoritative word of Jesus function as an
innerly persuasive word for the disciples? In other words, Why don't the
disciples fully embody Jesus' teaching, which exhorts them not to be
anxious (6.25-32; 10.19-33)? Instead, their anxiety comes to express the

51. Davies and Allison, *Matthew*, II, 73; Gundry, *Matthew*, 156; Edwards, *Portrait
of Disciples*, 35-37.
52. Davies and Allison, *Matthew*, II, 74.
53. Edwards, *Portrait of Disciples*, 31.

failure of the metaphorical seed, which proves unfruitful in the face of persecution (13.21) and worldly cares (13.22).

The analysis of aesthetic contemplation suggests an answer. In the first place, by not treating the readers' interaction with the disciples primarily as the means by which the author's values are conveyed to the readers, it becomes possible to characterize the disciples' role differently: rather than serving as the readers' principal link to the teaching of Jesus, the disciples can be seen more generally as those who are with Jesus, a characterization that subordinates their indisputable role as the principal recipients of his teaching. Evidence for this interpretation can be found in those passages that underscore the disciples' special relationship with Jesus: Jesus personally calls the disciples to follow him (4.18-22; 9.9), he instructs them apart from others (10.1-42; 13.10-23; 13.36-52; 18.1-35; 24.3–25.46), and he promises to be with them always (28.20; cf. 18.20). A striking example of the disciples' special relationship with Jesus occurs in the grainfields pericope (12.1-8): even though the disciples profane the Sabbath, they are pronounced guiltless, apparently for no reason other than that they are with Jesus, whose greatness, as Gundry observes, 'surpasses the sanctity of the Sabbath'.[54] The scriptural parallel of David's 'acceptable' violation of the Temple's sanctity—'and those who were with him' (12.3, 4)—confirms this interpretation.

Secondly, inasmuch as aesthetic contemplation accepts the limited perspective of the disciples as a component of reader–character interaction, it becomes clear that, despite their failure to understand, the disciples are nevertheless answerable for what has been given to them—a new status. On the other hand, the disciples' preoccupation with their own conception of their status in the company of Jesus not only suggests the difficulty of perceiving him through the veil of his ordinariness, but also implies that the life of discipleship represents an ongoing challenge to actualize this new life. Inasmuch as the disciples are never portrayed apart from their discipleship role, however, it becomes necessary to study the interactions between Jesus and the other character groups in order to learn what is missing in the disciples' response. In other words, the complete answer to the question of the disciples' shortcomings requires that we examine in particular the characterization of the supplicants, whose faith is commended by Jesus.

---

54. Gundry, *Matthew*, 223-24.

Chapter 5

THE SUPPLICANTS

The Narrative Role of the Supplicants

The failure of the disciples to embody fully the teaching of Jesus is all the more striking when one considers the paradigmatic faith response of such supplicants as the centurion (8.5-13) and the Canaanite woman (15.21-28): they are the only characters in Matthew's Gospel whose faith is characterized by Jesus as exemplary (8.10; 15.28), even though neither of them is a member of the character group the disciples. Although these and the other supplicants who exhibit faith in Matthew's Gospel are typically classified as minor characters who do not influence the plot of Matthew's story, gospel critics have nevertheless recognized their importance for establishing the readers' understanding of discipleship: when the limited faith response of the disciples is compared to the exemplary response of the supplicants, Matthew's definition of discipleship is said to be clarified for the readers. The role of the supplicants, in other words, as it is generally understood by gospel critics, essentially amounts to a way for the evangelist to communicate his discipleship values to the readers.

A Communication of Values

The redaction critic Heinz Held, for example, has observed that the failure on the part of the disciples to manifest adequate faith becomes the opportunity for Jesus to instruct the disciples on the true nature of faith, which *is* manifested by the supplicants. Held believes that the evangelist intends by this mixed portrayal of faith to address the needs of his community: 'little faith' is Matthew's designation for those who confess Jesus as the risen Lord, but who are unable to handle the pressure of the 'facts of this world' and therefore live a failed form of discipleship.[1] Consequently, Matthew's mixed portrayal of faith teaches his community, on the one hand, that a

---

1.   Held, 'Miracle Stories', 296.

broken form of faith, which is not yet unbelief, is not only possible within the community of believers, it in fact describes their condition. On the other hand, the evangelist's mixed portrayal of faith serves at the same time to assure his community that the Lord will respond to praying faith, just as he responded to the exemplary faith of the supplicants.[2] The discipleship value that Matthew apparently intends to communicate, according to Held's interpretation, is not only that steadfast, praying faith will be rewarded, but that such faith is characteristic of true discipleship.

Jack Kingsbury reaches a similar conclusion from his literary-critical perspective: he argues that the mixed portrayal of the disciples functions as an invitation for the readers to become 'schooled in the values that govern the life of discipleship in Matthew's story'.[3] Insofar as the disciples respond positively to Jesus, they are said to be like their teacher, a characterization that corresponds to Jesus' description of a disciple: 'It is sufficient for a disciple to be like his teacher' (10.25).[4] On the other hand, whenever the disciples fail to embody Jesus' teaching, manifesting fear or doubt instead of faith (8.26; 14.31; 17.20; 28.17), they show themselves to be at the same time unlike their teacher (26.39, 42), a characterization that serves to underscore their continued dependence upon him, or more specifically, upon his teaching.

Although Kingsbury does not thoroughly develop this line of reasoning, one possible implication of the positive characterization of the supplicants is that it enables Matthew to portray the intended discipleship response for the readers, which is manifested by the supplicants, while at the same time expressing the dependent teacher–disciple relationship of the disciples, which is shown to be effective only when occasions for teaching arise. This conclusion is compatible with Kingsbury's most explicit statements about the exemplary minor characters, which emphasize the role of the minor characters as the bearers of character traits 'that reflect the system of values that both Jesus and Matthew as narrator advocate'.[5] Another implication of this position is that discipleship comes to be viewed not as membership in the character group the disciples, but as the embodiment of all the values endorsed by the implied author, values that are fully embodied only in the implied reader.[6] In other words, according to this inter-

2. Held, 'Miracle Stories', 288.
3. Kingsbury, *Matthew as Story*, 13.
4. Kingsbury, *Matthew as Story*, 17.
5. Kingsbury, *Matthew as Story*, 27-28.
6. Howell, *Matthew's Inclusive Story*, 229-36.

pretation, discipleship is defined essentially as the proper response to Jesus,[7] regardless of the character's group membership. Consequently, Matthew's positive portrayal of the supplicants, who manifest the proper response to Jesus, is said to encourage the readers to identify with the supplicants, just as the implied reader initially identifies with the disciples. Unlike the disciples, however, these minor characters do not subsequently stumble. Therefore, their response to Jesus is said to be instructive for the implied reader, inasmuch as it embodies an aspect of discipleship that the disciples themselves are unable to manifest.

The readers' act of accepting the author's system of values, when framed in terms of the paradigmatic response of the supplicants, is conceived by these reading strategies essentially as a process of imitation that implicitly presupposes readers who have not previously endorsed the author's values. Certainly this is the presupposition of literary-critical approaches, which tend to emphasize the sequential-temporal flow of the reading experience, especially those approaches that rely on the first-time reader construct. In a sense, however, it is also the presupposition of the hypothetical reader implied by redaction criticism. Even though the historical readers of Matthew's community were likely to have been acquainted with the story[8] and already have endorsed its values, the redaction-critical analysis of the reader's interaction with the character group the supplicants, albeit limited, is virtually indistinguishable from the one proposed by literary critics: both the literary critics and the historical critics view the supplicants as exemplary characters who manifest traits as yet unattained by the readers. Yet if actual readers already concur with these values, then the proposal to describe the reader–character interaction in Matthew's Gospel primarily as a means of communicating the author's system of values, although certainly an acceptable interpretation, is incomplete as it stands. On the other hand, if the readers are in fact unable completely to embody their Lord's teaching, which is the narrative condition of the disciples, then it is possible that the Gospel is intended somehow to actualize the values of the text that otherwise remain unfulfilled, particularly on the part of those who already claim to accept them.

---

7.   Anderson, 'Gender and Reading', 16.

8.   Arguably, Matthew's historical readers were not only acquainted with the traditional story about Jesus—see Stanton, *Gospel*, 76—but, after the first reading, with Matthew's version of the story as well.

Great Faith and the Recognition of Need
The literary-critical approach of Kingsbury, Howell and others, despite correctly insisting on the contribution of all the character groups for the readers' apprehension of Matthew's definition of discipleship, nevertheless limits that contribution by privileging the implied reader's *evaluation* of the various responses of the character groups, which evaluation encourages the readers to identify with the positive characters and repudiate the negative ones. If, however, as some scholars have noted, the supplicants who manifest great faith are also individuals who are marginalized or otherwise in great need,[9] then it is possible that their great faith may be related to their need and the recognition of that need. If this is correct, then it is unlikely that the supplicants should be viewed solely as models of faith that the readers are invited to emulate. Rather, Matthew's characterization of the supplicants as those in need suggests that in order to actualize the great faith of the supplicants the readers must find themselves in the same condition as the supplicants, that is, they too must recognize that they are in need. According to this interpretation, the purpose of the supplicants' role in Matthew's Gospel is not solely to convey to the readers the example of persistent faith, which otherwise represents a straightforward communication of the author's discipleship values. Rather, it is also to embody the supplicants' faith response in the condition of need, a condition that is intensified by their status as outsiders, indeed the narrative's pre-eminent outsiders, neglected by the Jewish leadership, on the one hand, but never depicted as members of the character group the disciples, on the other hand.[10]

Need as the Defining Trait of the Supplicants

In order to establish that need—and the recognition of need—is the defining trait of Matthew's characterization of the supplicants, and therefore that the recognition of need should be a constitutive feature of the reader-supplicant interaction as well, we must first examine the theme of need in Matthew's Gospel as it relates to the characterization of the crowds, before analyzing the narrative's interactions between Jesus and the supplicants, in

9. See, for example, Anderson, 'Gender and Reading', 10-17, and Levine, *Matthean Salvation History*, 107-64.

10. Anderson, 'Gender and Reading', 17, suggests that 'the supplicants' function as foils would be limited if they became disciples'.

particular, the paradigmatic Gentile supplicants. Inasmuch as the supplicants are depicted as individual characters who emerge from the character group the crowds, their characterization to a considerable extent derives from their association with the crowds: it is the crowds who witness the miraculous healings of Jesus and hear his teaching; only when the supplicants approach Jesus individually does their characterization assume the traits that are specific to their particular situation.

Although the explicit need of the supplicants is for physical healing, whether for themselves (8.2; 9.21; 20.33) or for others (8.6; 9.18; 15.22), there is strong evidence that Matthew's stories of healing are intended primarily to serve an important symbolic function—to indicate the forgiveness of sins (9.6). This interpretation suggests that the need of the supplicants, as well as that of the crowds in general, is best understood not merely as the need for physical healing, but ultimately as the need for salvation from their sins.

The Need for Salvation from Sins
When an angel of the Lord appears to Joseph in a dream, the angel instructs Joseph to name the child Jesus, which name foreshadows the child's mission—'for he will save his people from their sins' (1.21). Inasmuch as Jesus is the most important character in Matthew's Gospel, whose relationship with the other characters is determinative of the readers' response to those characters, it stands to reason that salvation from sins not only defines the mission of Jesus, but also the need of the other characters with whom Jesus interacts, particularly the need of those who are his people.

Who are the people whom Jesus will save? The majority of commentators believe that the people of Jesus are his disciples, defined as the mixed community of Jews and Gentiles, his church (16.18), rather than the people of Israel, as might be inferred from the genealogy (1.2-17) and the missionary restriction (10.5-6; cf. 15.24).[11] Jesus' warning to the chief priests and Pharisees that 'the kingdom of God will be taken away from you and given to a nation producing the fruits of it' (21.43) is often cited as evidence supporting this interpretation.[12]

---

11. Gundry, *Matthew*, 23-24. On the other hand, Ulrich Luz, *Matthew 1–7: A Commentary* (trans. Wilhelm C. Linss; Minneapolis: Augsburg–Fortress, 1989), 105, argues that 'his people' refers to Israel.

12. Davies and Allison, *Matthew*, I, 210. Gundry cites additional examples of Matthew's apparent tendency to replace Israel with another community, including the

Although the commentators who identify Jesus' people with his church are certainly correct from a historical as well as a theological perspective, this mixed community of Jews and Gentiles is never explicitly defined as a character group in the Matthean narrative world.[13] Indeed, it is only at the end of the Gospel that the risen Lord lifts the restriction that limits the disciples' missionary activity to Israel (10.5-6), thereby inaugurating the age of the church (28.18-20). Ulrich Luz's interpretation, on the other hand, which equates Jesus' people with Israel,[14] better conforms to the frequently repeated observation that the narrative itself only recounts Jesus' mission to Israel: his encounters with the Gentiles, such as the centurion and the Canaanite woman, are presented as exceptional. Furthermore, not only does the mission of Jesus exclude the Gentiles, it apparently excludes the Jewish leadership as well: Jesus perceives himself as one who is sent 'only to the lost sheep of the house of Israel' (15.24; cf. 10.6). Inasmuch as the focus of Jesus' missionary activity in the narrative world of Matthew's Gospel is the crowds, clearly it is they who represent Israel's lost sheep (9.36), it is they who represent the people of Jesus.

The inaugural missionary activity of Jesus in Galilee, which is summarized in 4.23-25, according to Davies and Allison, 'characterizes not only Jesus' early work but his entire ministry'.[15] A comparison with the nearly identical summary in 9.35-37 supports this conclusion:

> And he went about all Galilee, teaching in their synagogues and preaching the gospel of the kingdom and healing every disease and every infirmity among the people. So his fame spread throughout all Syria, and they brought him all the sick, those afflicted with various diseases and pains, demoniacs, epileptics, and paralytics, and he healed them. And great crowds

substitution of 'Israel' with 'his people' in Ps. 130.8, the text quoted by the angel to explain the significance of the name Jesus; and the shifting of 'forgiveness of sins' from John's baptism of repentance (Mk 1.4; cf. Mt. 3.1-2) to the Words of Institution (Mt. 26.28; cf. Mk 14.24).

13. References to the church do not constitute a character group. Richard E. Menninger, *Israel and the Church in the Gospel of Matthew* (New York: Peter Lang, 1994), 167, concedes 'that Matthew did not compose his gospel primarily in order to prove the church as the true Israel—his intent was to show Jesus as the Messiah of Israel'. Nevertheless, he concludes that there is considerable evidence 'to suggest that Matthew repeatedly writes in a way that *reflects* [emphasis added] his belief that the church *is* [emphasis in original] the true Israel' (167).

14. Luz, *Matthew 1–7*, 105.

15. Davies and Allison, *Matthew*, I, 412.

followed him from Galilee and the Decapolis and Jerusalem and Judea and from beyond the Jordan (4.23-25).

> And Jesus went about all the cities and villages, teaching in their syna-
> gogues and preaching the gospel of the kingdom, and healing every disease
> and every infirmity. When he saw the crowds, he had compassion for them,
> because they were harassed and helpless, like sheep without a shepherd.
> Then he said to his disciples, 'The harvest is plentiful, but the laborers are
> few; pray therefore the Lord of the harvest to send out laborers into his
> harvest' (9.35-37).

Together these summaries establish the characteristics of Jesus' public ministry: (1) he seeks out the crowds (4.23; 9.35); (2) he teaches, preaches and heals (4.23; 9.35); (3) he acts out of 'compassion' for the crowds,[16] recognizing that they are leaderless, 'harassed and helpless, like sheep without a shepherd' (9.36); (4) although he begins his ministry by seeking out the crowds, eventually, as his fame spreads, the word of his activity causes the crowds to bring their sick to Jesus in order to be healed by him (4.24); and (5) subsequently, the crowds follow him (4.25).

The emphasis on healing in the summaries of Jesus' ministry might seem surprising in view of the explicit missionary intention of Jesus to save the people from their sins. It appears, however, that Matthew intends Jesus' healing miracles to be perceived as signs of the messianic age, a time of anticipated forgiveness.[17] For example, when the imprisoned John the Baptist sends his disciples to ask Jesus if he is the Christ, Jesus responds by reminding them of what they have seen and heard: '…the blind receive their sight and the lame walk, lepers are cleansed and the deaf hear, and the dead are raised up, and the poor have good news preached to them' (11.5). Such a response by Jesus makes sense only in the light of messianic expectations, which, while difficult to establish historically,[18] are clearly presupposed by the text.

The theme of salvation from sins, while implicitly underlying Matthew's interpretation of the miraculous deeds of Jesus the messiah, is explicitly

---

16. The theme of compassion is reiterated later, when it is linked again to healing: 'As he went ashore he saw a great throng; and he had compassion on them, and healed their sick' (14.14).

17. Davies and Allison, *Matthew*, II, 90, cite CD 14.19 and 11QMelch 4–9 as evidence of the anticipated forgiveness of the messianic age.

18. Davies and Allison, *Matthew*, II, 90, while acknowledging that the messianic age was expected to bring forgiveness, find no clear evidence 'that the Messiah himself was expected to intercede or atone for sins'.

linked to miracle in the account of Jesus' healing of the paralytic (9.1-8). When the paralytic is brought to Jesus for healing, an encounter that concretizes the pattern of the Galilean missionary summary (4.24), Jesus pronounces his sins forgiven, rather than immediately fulfilling his implicit petition to be healed physically. Only after the condemnatory reaction of the scribes and Pharisees does Jesus heal the paralytic's infirmity, thereby establishing that he has the authority to forgive sins as well. The choral response of the crowds confirms this interpretation: 'When the crowds saw it, they were afraid, and they glorified God, who had given such authority to men' (9.8). Arguably, therefore, all of the accounts of healing in Matthew's Gospel can be viewed as symbolizing the forgiveness of sins.[19]

Teaching, Preaching, Healing and Forgiveness

As the word of Jesus' activity spreads, it causes the crowds to bring their sick to Jesus in order to be healed by him: 'So his fame spread throughout all Syria, and they brought him all the sick, those afflicted with various diseases and pains, demoniacs, epileptics, and paralytics, and he healed them' (4.24). On the basis of the Galilean missionary summary it is possible to conclude that the miraculous healings of Jesus are responsible for attracting the crowds. Such an inference can also be supported by the account of Jesus' condemnation of the cities Chorazin and Bethsaida, where Jesus rebukes the people for failing to repent at his preaching, despite the evidence of the mighty works that he performed there (11.20-21). Mighty works, however, are not unambiguous; they must be properly interpreted. For example, when Jesus casts out demons, he is accused by his opponents of colluding with Beelzebul (12.24). Although from the evangelist's perspective the Beelzebul accusation against Jesus is a false charge, it is not an impossible one: Jesus himself warns his disciples that false Christs and false prophets will perform 'great signs and wonders, so as to lead astray, if possible, even the elect' (24.24). And indeed, the (false) prophets who perform mighty works in the name of Jesus are con-

---

19. In a similar vein, Keener, *Matthew*, 289, argues that '[a]lthough Jesus' miracles teach about his power to heal physically, these signs are especially meant to turn attention to the kingdom of God (6.33; 9.12)'. Perhaps the clearest example of the symbolic function of the healing miracles is the healing of the two blind men (20.29-34): Via, *Self-Deception*, 108, noting that sight is an image of understanding (13.14-17), argues that the healing of the blind men, inasmuch as it occurs immediately after the ransom saying (20.28), 'interprets the death of Jesus as saving the many by conferring the understanding necessary for ethical fruitfulness (13.23)'.

demned at the judgment, because they did not do the will of God (7.21-23). The possibility of misinterpreting the purpose of the messianic signs therefore suggests that more than the signs themselves is needed for proper understanding. As we learn from the parable of the wise man who builds his house upon the rock (7.24-27), it is only the faithful adherence to the words of Jesus that will ensure the correct understanding of miracles in the messianic age.

Therefore, although it is certainly possible, as Davies and Allison believe, that 'Jesus' fame was undoubtedly largely due to his powers as a wonder-worker',[20] the report of his activity should not be understood, in Matthew's narrative world, to refer exclusively to his miraculous deeds, but should include his preaching and teaching as well. Indeed, the Gospel's general interest in presenting Jesus as the teacher, which interest has arguably even shaped the wording of the missionary summary,[21] suggests that Matthew intends the teaching of Jesus to be understood as the principal means by which Jesus conveys divine forgiveness.[22] By so emphasizing the teaching of Jesus, Matthew fulfills the prophecy of Jeremiah, which establishes a correspondence between the forgiveness of sins and the eschatological knowledge of the law (Jer. 31.31-34).

Sheep without a Shepherd
Israel's need for the eschatological knowledge of the law helps to explain Matthew's characterization of the crowds, which includes both positive and negative traits, a characterization that is not unlike the mixed characterization of the disciples. On the one hand, as Kingsbury notes, the crowds are generally positive, inasmuch as when they interact with Jesus they are for the most part 'well-disposed toward him'.[23] On the other hand, however, their failure to realize that Jesus is more than a prophet exemplifies a negative trait: they are 'without faith in Jesus'.[24] Nevertheless, Jesus himself characterizes the crowds as 'harassed and helpless, like sheep without a shepherd' (9.36), which characterization expresses his compassion for them rather than his condemnation.

20. Davies and Allison, *Matthew*, I, 416.
21. Gundry, *Matthew*, 63, contends that the evangelist places the participle 'teaching' in first place to emphasize the teaching of Jesus.
22. Patte, *Matthew*, 389, argues that the death of Jesus enables people to recognize his words and acts as a revelation from God; they are saved 'by doing his teaching'.
23. Kingsbury, *Matthew as Story*, 24.
24. Kingsbury, *Matthew as Story*, 24.

The compassionate response of Jesus in this situation suggests that the blame for the condition of the crowds lies not with the crowds themselves, but with their leaders, even though it is the crowds who accept the responsibility for the execution of Jesus, an innocent man (27.24-25). In other words, the mixed characterization of the crowds should be viewed as an expression of their helplessness, rather than as one of the author's means of conveying values that are to be rejected by the readers. This is because, as we shall see, the helplessness of the crowds is a consequence of their leaders' failure to fulfill their role as the teachers of the law.

Implicitly, the responsibility in Matthew's Gospel for the well-being of the crowds belongs to the Jewish leaders, among whom the Pharisees occupy a prominent role. On the one hand, the chief priests and elders have sufficient authority over the crowds to send them to seize Jesus (26.47) and then persuade them to seek his crucifixion (27.20), apparently the same crowds that earlier had greeted Jesus as the Son of David (21.8-11) and daily heard his teaching in the temple (26.55). These leaders, however, lack compassion for the crowds, seeking instead their own benefit: even Pilate himself recognizes that Jesus is delivered up out of the leaders' envy (27.18), clearly a self-serving motivation.

Not only do the chief priests and elders fail to express compassion for the crowds, but they actually fear the crowds, which is yet another expression of the self-concern that determines their conduct toward the people. When Jesus asks the chief priests and elders to name the authority of John's baptism, they refuse to answer him, admitting to themselves that they fear the crowds (21.26), who hold John to be a prophet. Likewise, when Jesus tells the parable of the vineyard against the chief priests and Pharisees, these leaders abandon their immediate plan to arrest Jesus, again because they fear the crowds (21.46), who also hold Jesus to be a prophet.

The Jewish leaders' fear of the crowds is not only an expression of their self-concern, it is also an indication that they have forsaken their role as leaders. Even what little authority over the people the Jewish leaders seem to possess, such as when they send the crowds to arrest Jesus (26.47), is further mitigated by the fact that to accomplish their purpose they must *persuade* the people to ask for Jesus' death before the governor (27.20).

The strongest evidence that the Jewish leaders have abandoned their responsibility for the people, however, is their failure to teach the people the will of God. On the one hand, the Jewish leaders' knowledge of God's will is certain: the scribes and (chief priests) are able to search the

Scriptures, correctly telling Herod that the Christ is to be born in Bethle-
hem (2.4-6). On the other hand, their knowledge of the Scriptures alone is
not sufficient: ironically, having used the Scriptures to discover the
birthplace of the Christ, Herod uses this information to serve his own purpose, which is to seek the child's death (2.13, 16).

In Matthew's Gospel the responsibility to teach the people clearly
belongs to the scribes and Pharisees: on the one hand, the scribes' teaching
responsibility can be inferred from the crowds' positive reception of the
teaching of Jesus, who 'taught them as one who had authority, and not as
their scribes' (7.29); on the other hand, the responsibility to teach the people is also directly ascribed to the scribes and Pharisees by Jesus himself,
who insists that they rightly occupy the teaching chair of Moses, only
warning his listeners that his opponents do not practice what they teach
(23.2-3). In light of Jesus' earlier warning to his disciples to beware of the
leaven of the Pharisees (and Sadducees), which warning Jesus himself
understands to refer to their teaching (16.12), it is unlikely that Matthew is
referring in 23.3 to a contradiction between what the Pharisees say and do
in general, as some commentators have concluded.[25] After all, as Gundry
notes, the scribes and Pharisees do keep their own traditions.[26] If, on the
other hand, one understands the reference to Moses' chair as a qualifying
reference, which is intended to exclude the interpretive traditions of the
scribes and Pharisees,[27] then it is more likely that Jesus' condemnation of
the scribes and Pharisees stems from their failure to keep the law as Jesus
himself interprets it. In other words, since the scribes and Pharisees are
said to keep their traditions and not the law (15.3-6), their practice is to be
avoided. Jesus' subsequent charge that the scribes and Pharisees lay heavy
burdens on others (23.4) appears to tie their practice to the burdensome
praise that they expect from others (23.5-7).[28] Consequently, the compas-

25. For example, Davies and Allison, *Matthew*, III, 270-71, argue that in light of
the rhetorical hyperbole of Mt. 23 it is possible to conclude that the scribes and
Pharisees are being criticized for their inconsistencies: they 'are not criticized for
having the wrong tradition but for not living according to the tradition they confess'.
Davies and Allison cite as additional evidence the widespread use of the hypocrisy
charge in ancient polemics to label one's opponents.

26. Gundry, *Matthew*, 455. Although Gundry does not cite examples of the scribes
and Pharisees keeping their own traditions, one can infer their faithful adherence from
Jesus' charge that the Pharisees transgress the commandment of God for the sake of
their tradition (15.3-9).

27. So Gundry, *Matthew*, 455.

28. Gundry, *Matthew*, 455-56.

sion that the scribes and Pharisees fail to exhibit, by not moving the heavy burdens with a finger (23.4), is their refusal to remove the burden of praise. By failing to remove this burden, they are said to abdicate their role as leaders.

Jesus and the Gentile Supplicants

Israel's need for divine forgiveness and the eschatological knowledge of the law, which the mission of Jesus is intended to actualize, constitutes the need of all of the characters who approach Jesus in the narrative world of Matthew's Gospel, including the Gentile supplicants whose interaction with Jesus is depicted as exceptional. Just like the lost sheep of Israel, whose need for physical healing is symbolic of their greater need for forgiveness and existential understanding, so also is the need of the Gentile supplicants. Although the characterization of the supplicants as those who emerge from the (Jewish) crowds is much clearer in the case of the Jewish supplicants, such as the leper (8.1-4), the woman with a hemorrhage (9.20-22), and the two blind men (20.29-34), I intend to concentrate on the role of the Gentile supplicants, whose status as the narrative's pre-eminent outsiders introduces an aspect of need that is missing from the characterization of the neglected people of Israel. Although the Gentile supplicants ultimately seek the fulfillment of the same need as the people of Israel, their status as outsiders (cf. 18.17) serves to underscore the unworthiness of their supplication, which unworthiness is manifested in their extended dialogue with Jesus.

Matthew 8.5-13

Davies and Allison argue that the significance of the centurion in 8.5-13 is twofold: first, that he is a Gentile, who 'foreshadows (as did the magi) the successful evangelization of the nations (28.16-20)'; and secondly, that his faith is paradigmatic for the believer, as one who 'trusts implicitly in Jesus' power and authority'.[29] Such faith, Davies and Allison conclude, 'conquers the separation between Jew and Gentile',[30] an implicit acknowledgment of the centurion's status as an outsider who has no claim on the mission of Jesus. Omitted in the analysis of Davies and Allison, however, is any discussion of the centurion's understanding of his outsider status. In accordance with Richard Edwards's scheme, which identifies five narrative

29. Davies and Allison, *Matthew*, II, 19.
30. Davies and Allison, *Matthew*, II, 25.

features that enable the readers to recognize the traits of a character,[31] the
self-understanding of the centurion can reasonably be inferred from a combination of the centurion's own words, Jesus' words about the Gentiles in
general, and Jesus' words to the centurion in particular.

The centurion's first words to Jesus—'Lord, my servant is lying para-
lyzed at home, in terrible distress' (8.6)—imply the centurion's recognition
of a need that he himself is unable to fulfill. Inasmuch as the centurion is
said to approach Jesus as he enters Capernaum, the center of Jesus'
Galilean ministry (4.13; cf. 9.1),[32] it would appear that the circulating
word about Jesus, which includes both miracle and teaching (4.23-25), is
responsible for bringing the centurion to faith.[33] Although little can be said
about the centurion's understanding of Jesus and his teaching, Birger
Gerhardsson's comment that the supplicants in general, whenever they
address Jesus as Lord, are 'on the right track without realizing anything
like the whole truth about Jesus',[34] does not ring true for Matthew's narrative world, one in which the centurion's paradigmatic faith, unlike Peter's
confession on the road to Caesarea Philippi (16.16), does not subsequently
prove to be inadequate (cf. 16.23).

Jesus' reply to the centurion (8.7), which the RSV translates as a statement of compliance ('I will come and heal him'), can also be translated as
a question implying resistance ('Should I coming heal him?'). Davies and
Allison argue for the latter translation, citing in particular the story's similarity to the story of the Canaanite woman (15.21-28), in which 'a Gentile's request for her daughter's healing is initially met with a negative
response'.[35] Gundry, on the other hand, rejects this type of reasoning,
arguing instead that the emphasis in Jesus' direct discourse falls on his
authority to heal, not on the rebuff of a Gentile.[36] Consequently, according
to Gundry, the astonishment in this story does not belong to an indignant
Jesus, but to the centurion, who is surprised that a Jew would be willing to

31. Edwards, *Portrait of Disciples*, 12-13.

32. Davies and Allison, *Matthew*, I, 378, suggest that the city Capernaum, which
may have been an important city in Matthew's tradition, is emphasized by the evangelist 'because of its location in the territory named in Isaiah's prophecy (9.1-2)'.

33. Via, *Self-Deception*, 99.

34. Birger Gerhardsson, *The Mighty Acts of Jesus According to Matthew* (trans.
Robert Dewsnap; Lund: C.W.K. Gleerup, 1979), 86. Cited approvingly by Davies and
Allison, *Matthew*, II, 20.

35. Davies and Allison, *Matthew*, II, 22.

36. Gundry, *Matthew*, 143.

fulfill his request by coming to his house, thereby contracting ceremonial defilement.

It is, of course, impossible to be certain which of these interpretations expresses the intention of the evangelist; nevertheless, the difference between the two, upon closer examination, does not appear to be significant for the purpose of determining the self-understanding of the centurion. This is because the subsequent words of the centurion, which express his recognition that he is not worthy to have Jesus come to his house (8.8), imply that the negative attitude toward the Gentiles, which is evident in the Gospel's narrative world (5.47; 6.7; 10.5; 15.24; 18.17), is also determinative of the centurion's self-understanding: not only does the centurion implicitly know that he is powerless to fulfill his own need, he also appears to understand that he has no right to make his supplication. Consequently, the reader of aesthetic contemplation, who holds together the limited perspective of the character and the finalizing perspective of the author, must also encounter the Lord from the outsider's perspective of the centurion, uncertain that Jesus will fulfill the centurion's request. Partly this is due to the nature of requests in general, which imply the possibility that the petitioner might be rejected. More importantly, it is due to the fact that the centurion does not know what the reader of aesthetic contemplation knows—that Jesus will not only fulfill his request, but that the risen Lord will send his disciples to baptize and teach all the nations (28.18-20), thereby overcoming the separation between Jew and Gentile.

Although it is implied that the circulating word about Jesus has brought the centurion to faith, in accordance with the pattern of the missionary summary (4.24), it is not until *after* the response of Jesus in 8.7 that the centurion's exemplary faith is manifested: 'Lord, I am not worthy to have you come under my roof; but only say the word and my servant will be healed' (8.8). This suggests that it is the words of Jesus that are responsible for eliciting the centurion's exemplary response. Therefore, whether the words of Jesus are thought to indicate compliance or resistance, they achieve the same result: they establish that the centurion understands his unworthiness.

The centurion's recognition of his unworthiness is expressed as a type of self-lowering, wherein a Gentile soldier who has others under his authority makes supplication of Jesus, the carpenter's son (13.55). Therefore, when the reader of aesthetic contemplation approaches Jesus from the perspective of the centurion, he does so as the (relatively) high status

Gentile who approaches not the risen Lord but the carpenter's son. What the reader of aesthetic contemplation ultimately understands, however, is that to make supplication of the carpenter's son, which is an act of self-lowering, is at the same time to make supplication of the Lord himself. This self-lowering on the part of the centurion recalls for the reader of aesthetic contemplation the private instructions of Jesus to his disciples that they should take up their crosses (10.38; 16.24), lose their lives (10.39; 16.25), humble themselves like a child (18.3-4), and become the servants of others (20.26-27). In other words, it is a self-lowering that actualizes the pattern established by Jesus himself, who takes up his own cross (20.19), loses his own life (16.21, 23; 20.28) and comes to serve others rather than be served himself (20.28), which pattern represents the will of his Father (26.39, 42), who raises Jesus from the dead (16.9, 23).

Matthew 15.21-28

While it is debated whether the words of Jesus to the centurion (8.7) should be interpreted as a statement of compliance or a question of resistance, commentators generally agree that Jesus' reply to the Canaanite woman—'It is not fair to take the children's bread and throw it to the dogs' (15.26)—represents a rejection of the woman's supplication, which rejection only serves to highlight her great faith (15.27).[37] Commentators differ, on the other hand, regarding the severity of Jesus' rebuff. Gundry, for one, suggests that Jesus has in mind household pets, a softening that conceivably would reduce the possibility of interpreting Jesus' words with an anti-Gentile bias.[38] David Garland, on the other hand, argues that despite the use of the diminutive form of 'dogs', the text does nothing to diminish the harshness of Jesus' response: 'A dog is a dog whether it is a pampered household pet or a street cur.'[39] Indeed, the final appeal of the Canaanite woman overcomes what is arguably the harshest in an series of apparently increasingly harsh responses by Jesus: the woman's initial appeal is met with silence (15.23), her subsequent supplication, which is implied in the disciples' request that Jesus send her away, provokes Jesus to respond that he was sent 'only to the lost sheep of the house of Israel' (15.24), while her third appeal provokes Jesus to say that 'it is not fair to take the children's bread and throw it to the dogs' (15.26), which response

---

37. Gundry, *Matthew*, 314; Davies and Allison, *Matthew*, II, 552.
38. Gundry, *Matthew*, 316.
39. Garland, *Reading Matthew*, 165.

implicitly correlates the woman's status to that of the dogs who are undeserving of the children's bread.

Regardless of how one interprets the severity of Jesus' rejection of the Canaanite woman, it is clear that she accepts Jesus' implicit characterization of her status: 'Yes, Lord, yet even the dogs eat the crumbs that fall from their master's table' (15.27). Furthermore, it is precisely the Canaanite woman's acceptance of Jesus' characterization of her status, her final appeal, that is considered to be the manifestation of great faith (15.28). Like the centurion, the Canaanite woman overcomes the objection of Jesus' response, expressing the recognition of her need in the face of her unworthiness. Unlike the centurion, on the other hand, a relatively high status character who manifests his faith in an act of self-lowering, the Canaanite woman is depicted as a thoroughly marginalized character, whose great faith is manifested in the very acknowledgment of her low status. Janice Capel Anderson, arguing partly on the basis of a feminist hermeneutic, has even described the status of the Canaanite woman, who is both a Gentile and a woman, as doubly marginal.[40] And indeed, the marginalization of the Canaanite woman *qua* woman in a patriarchal society may well be implied by the fact that she herself is the one who makes the supplication: the Canaanite woman is the only female character in Matthew's Gospel who makes supplication on behalf of another, whether a servant (8.5-13) or a dependent child (9.18-26; 15.21-28; 17.14-18), which implies that she herself is a widow.

When the reader of aesthetic contemplation approaches Jesus from the perspective of the Canaanite woman, she is confronted with a challenge similar to the one posed by the centurion's perspective: the reader of aesthetic contemplation makes supplication of the carpenter's son momentarily without the benefit of the post-resurrection declaration that he is also the risen Lord, to whom 'All authority on heaven and earth has been given' (28.18). Nevertheless, she approaches Jesus confident that he can fulfill her request, which confidence is implied by her very act of supplication, but at the same time uncertain that he will actually do so. In other words, the sequential-temporal flow of the narrative, which approximates the character's limited perspective in the definition of the reader of aesthetic contemplation, establishes the perspective of unmerited, uncertain supplication, an aspect of the Canaanite woman's need that cannot easily be imitated, especially by readers whose understanding has already been

40. Anderson, 'Gender and Reading', 11.

formed by the conviction that the risen Lord fulfills the petitions of his supplicants. Ultimately, therefore, the reader of aesthetic contemplation is challenged to recognize that she is powerless to fulfill her own need, which the reader of aesthetic contemplation understands from the author's finalizing perspective is symbolic of the need for divine forgiveness and the eschatological knowledge of the law. The unique contribution of the Canaanite woman, when compared to the centurion's encounter with Jesus, is that she accepts Jesus' characterization of her unworthiness. In Bakhtin's terminology, the authoritative word of Jesus is accepted by the Canaanite woman as an internally persuasive word, a rare conjunction, according to Bakhtin, in which the authoritative word of Jesus is said literally to constitute the Canaanite woman's own word about herself.

The Potentiality of Need
The role of the Gentile supplicants in Matthew's Gospel, which apparently is intended to embody both the need of the supplicants as well as their great faith, arguably manifests need as the condition of emptiness, which is expressed as the centurion's relinquishing of his high status or the Canaanite woman's acceptance of her low status. This interpretation of the role of the Gentile supplicants in turn raises the question, What is the relationship between need, specifically manifested as emptiness, and great faith? The short answer is that emptiness establishes the potentiality of being filled.

Dan Via's structuralist interpretation of Matthew's Beatitudes (5.3-10) develops a convincing argument for understanding the recognition of need in Matthew's Gospel as the condition of potentiality to be filled.[41] Via begins his analysis by demonstrating that the Beatitudes are formed on the basis of tight structural equivalences, both individually and as a whole. Individually, each Beatitude is composed of two related clauses: a declaration of blessedness and its grounding, understood as a present affirmation or a future promise. As a whole, the Beatitudes are presented in two related groups of four members: the first group paradoxically combines blessedness with emptiness or the lack of positive qualities, Via's characterization of poor in spirit, mourners, meek, and hungering for righteousness;[42] the

41. Via, *Self-Deception*, 123-27.
42. Via, *Self-Deception*, counters the tendency to view these qualities solely in a positive light, as virtues to be achieved, such as humility, in the case of poverty of spirit. Citing Matthew's use of spirit in the Gethsemane scene (28.41), Via argues that spirit should be understood as 'the seat of willingness to be faithful and loyal' (125).

second group, on the other hand, combines blessedness with fullness or the achievement of positive qualities, Via's characterization of merciful, pure in heart, peacemakers and persecuted for righteousness. The structural equivalences of the Beatitudes bind together the qualities of emptiness and fullness in the first clauses, which suggests that emptiness can be understood as the potentiality for fullness. The second clauses of the Beatitudes, which define the grounding of blessing in terms of the kingdom heaven, establish a similar potentiality by defining the kingdom as both a present and future reality, one in which the presence of the kingdom represents both actualization and potentiality: 'That the kingdom is present means that emptiness has been filled, that possibility has become actuality. But since the kingdom is also future, the present as actuality is turned into potentiality for further actualization in the future.'[43]

The mere potentiality of emptiness, however, does not ensure its own actualization. As Via argues, 'the positive potentiality of emptiness is contingent upon recognizing oneself as empty'.[44] Paradoxically, this means that even after emptiness has been filled by the presence of the kingdom, which in Matthew's Gospel can be understood as the granting of forgiveness and the eschatological knowledge of the law, one must nevertheless still recognize oneself as empty in order that the kingdom's presence might serve as the new potentiality for further actualization in the future. This means, as Via argues, that '[w]hat God gives is not a fixed possession but a dialectical movement. Thus it can slip away just when one thinks one has it.'[45] Fullness, in other words, can have the unintended effect of preventing one from seeing that one is, in a deeper sense, actually empty. The parable of the unforgiving servant (18.23-35), who squanders the king's unexpected beneficence, exemplifies the dialectical nature of the kingdom's presence, its potentiality for further actualization.

The Gentile supplicants in Matthew's Gospel are said to be paradigmatic for Matthew's readers because they manifest great faith. Yet it is clear that their great faith is related to their recognition of need, which in the case of the Gentile supplicants is ultimately manifested as the relinquishing of high status or the acceptance of low status. Although there is a sense in which the recognition of need serves as the precondition for the

---

Therefore, poverty of spirit is 'a lack of will to faithfulness', a thoroughly negative quality.

43. Via, *Self-Deception*, 126.
44. Via, *Self-Deception*, 127.
45. Via, *Self-Deception*, 127.

actualization of potentiality, it is also clear that it is the word of Jesus that enables the supplicants to recognize their need in the first place: the circulating word about Jesus initially brings the supplicants to Jesus, while his subsequent word evokes their paradigmatic faith response. Arguably, therefore, in order for the readers to actualize the potentiality of need, they must find themselves in the same condition as the Gentile supplicants, a condition of need that cannot simply be imitated. For the readers of Matthew's Gospel, this means that the Gospel itself not only must ultimately fill their need, but it must also create the condition of need in the first place. Otherwise, the readers of Matthew's Gospel, like the character group the disciples, who fail to actualize the pattern of Jesus' life despite repeatedly hearing his teaching, will never become the fruitful receivers of his word. It is the argument of this study that Matthew's Gospel establishes the readers in the condition of need by casting them in the role of the Pharisees, who are the principal opponents of Jesus in Matthew's narrative world.

Chapter 6

THE PHARISEES

The Narrative Role of the Pharisees

The principal opponents of Jesus in Matthew's Gospel are the character group the Jewish leaders, a group comprising the chief priests, the elders, the Sadduccees, the scribes and the Pharisees. Despite the distinctions in their respective characterizations,[1] Kingsbury argues that inasmuch as the rhetorical effect of the Gospel's presentation of these individual groups essentially makes of them a 'united front opposed to Jesus', it is possible to treat them as a single character group.[2] By treating these characters as a single group, Kingsbury is able to ascribe the traits of individual characters or groups of characters to the character group the Jewish leaders as a whole. Therefore, when John the Baptist denounces the Pharisees and Sadducees as a 'brood of vipers' (3.7), which epithet characterizes them as evil, Kingsbury concludes that 'evilness' is the root trait of the Jewish leaders as a whole,[3] even though the other members of the group are never explicitly characterized as a brood of vipers.[4] Similarly, Kingsbury considers 'hypocrisy' to be a trait that is characteristic of the Jewish leaders as a whole, even though it is primarily used to define an attribute of the Pharisees, whether alone (22.18) or together with the scribes (15.7; 23.13, 15, 23, 25, 27, 28, 29).

As the opponents of Jesus, the Jewish leaders are the character group most responsible for advancing the plot of Matthew's narrative: not only

---

1. Kingsbury, *Matthew as Story*, 18-19, notes that whereas the chief priests and elders are associated more with Jerusalem and the temple, the scribes and Pharisees are linked to the synagogues and associated with the law and the tradition of the elders.

2. Kingsbury, *Matthew as Story*, 18. So also, Howell, *Matthew's Inclusive Story*, 236.

3. Kingsbury, *Matthew as Story*, 19.

4. The epithet 'brood of vipers' is used elsewhere of the Pharisees (12.34) and the scribes and Pharisees (23.33).

do they test Jesus (16.1; 19.3; 22.35), they plot to destroy him (12.14), they try to arrest him openly, only to abandon their plans for fear of the crowds (21.46), they send a great crowd to arrest him secretly at night (26.47-56), they preside over his trial, seeking false testimony to convict him (26.57-68), they deliver him to Pilate to be put to death (27.1-2), they persuade the people to ask for the release of Barabbas and the crucifixion of Jesus (27.20-23), and finally they convince Pilate to set a guard at the sepulcher of Jesus, thereby attempting to forestall the anticipated announcement of his resurrection (27.62-66).

With respect to the problem of reader–character interaction, the Jewish leaders' opposition to Jesus, 'God's supreme agent who is in complete accord with God's system of values',[5] is indicative of a value system that is rejected by the implied author of Matthew's Gospel. Therefore, gospel critics have recognized the importance of the Jewish leaders as foils for discipleship: when the negative response of the Jewish leaders is compared to the exemplary response of the supplicants and the positive, albeit limited, response of the disciples, Matthew's definition of discipleship is said to be clarified for the readers. The characterization of the Jewish leaders as the opponents of Jesus clarifies the true nature of Matthean discipleship by establishing a negative example for the readers, which example is 'antithetical to the value system and virtues which Jesus calls his followers to display and which fully characterize his own life'.[6] The negative portrayal of the Jewish leaders is said to encourage the readers to repudiate them and, therefore, their value system as well.[7]

Value System of the Jewish Leaders

Gospel critics typically reconstruct the value system of the Jewish leaders, or their ideological point of view, from the evidence of their behavior and their teaching, often as reported by others. Howell, for example, derives the value system of the Jewish leaders essentially from Jesus' characterization of them as recorded in the woes against the scribes and Pharisees.

---

5. Kingsbury, *Matthew as Story*, 11.

6. Howell, *Matthew's Inclusive Story*, 237.

7. Luke T. Johnson, 'The New Testament's Anti-Jewish Slander and the Conventions of Ancient Polemic', *JBL* 108 (1989), 419-41, argues that the slander topos was used in Greco-Roman rhetoric to distance the addressees from the teaching of opposing philosophical schools.

According to Howell,

> The Jewish leaders do not practice what they preach, and they perform acts of piety ostentatiously in order to be praised by other (23.3-5; cf. 6.1-6, 16-18). As religious leaders of Israel, they shut entry into the Kingdom instead of providing access to it (23.13-15). They display blindness about the Law (cf. 15.1-10), their teaching on oaths distorts the meaning of sacred things (23.16-22), and the weightier matters of the Law are neglected while their observance of insignificant things is scrupulous (23.23-24; cf. 12.1-8). The Jewish leaders may thus appear outwardly righteous, but inwardly they are full of hypocrisy and lawlessness (23.27-28). In short, they fail to do the will of God.[8]

The readers' response, based on this description of the Jewish leaders' value system, presumably would be to renounce ostentatious piety, provide others access to the kingdom of heaven, and attend to the weightier matters of the law.

While the rejection of the Jewish leaders and their value system is arguably present as an intention of the text, there are, however, certain difficulties with this interpretation. First, the literary-critical approach of Howell and Kingsbury fails to address the problem of the readers who have already endorsed the author's values but nevertheless continue to be addressed by the text. If the readers already concur with these values, in this case by rejecting the value system of the Jewish leaders, then the attempt to describe the reader–character interaction in Matthew's Gospel primarily as the communication of a system of values is incomplete. Howell's explanation that actual readers are called to correct themselves in light of the Gospel's system of values[9] fails to address the problem that readers who are not directly confronted with their shortcomings, a characteristic of reading strategies that view reader–character interaction primarily as a means of communicating values, may be more inclined to judge others than to correct themselves (cf. 7.1-5).

The second problem with the approach of Howell and Kingsbury is that it does not consider the possibility that the ideological point of view of the Jewish leaders would likely be valued quite differently by the Jewish leaders themselves, who undoubtedly would take exception to Jesus' negative characterization of them. In other words, it is unlikely that the Jewish leaders would view themselves as those who perform ostentatious acts of piety (23.5), block the admission of others into the kingdom of heaven

---

8.   Howell, *Matthew's Inclusive Story*, 237.
9.   Howell, *Matthew's Inclusive Story*, 247.

(23.13), at least not without a proper cause, and neglect the weightier matters of the law (23.23). Clearly, therefore, there is an implicit contradiction between the self-evaluation of the Jewish leaders, so defined, and Jesus' authoritative evaluation of the Jewish leaders.

The model of communication underlying the approach of Howell and Kingsbury, however, a model that privileges the communication of values inferred primarily from character traits, fails to identify, and is therefore unable to define a function for, the Jewish leaders' implicit, positive self-evaluation. Bakhtin's 'model' of aesthetic contemplation, on the other hand, not only acknowledges all of the self-manifestations of the Jewish leaders, assembling them into a concrete whole of meaning, it accepts all of them, whether good or evil, which acceptance is necessary if the readers truly are to be engaged by the narrative role that is defined by the Jewish leaders.

The challenge of a Bakhtinian analysis, therefore, is to study the interaction between Jesus and the Jewish leaders without reducing the Jewish leaders to a paradigm of traits that serves merely as the expression of a repudiated value system. Kingsbury's categorization of the various opponents of Jesus as a monolithic group, however, tends to reinforce the perception that they should be viewed precisely as such a paradigm. Only by studying the opponents of Jesus individually, as they interact with Jesus in the various narrative scenes of Matthew's Gospel, is one able to recognize the dialogic nature of character interaction.

Pharisees as the Main Opponents

Although there are a number of scenes in Matthew's Gospel in which Jesus is confronted by his opponents, only a few of these scenes depict Jesus as characterizing his opponents by means of an encompassing definition, as expressed by the epithets 'brood of vipers' (12.34; 23.33), 'hypocrites' (15.7; 22.18; 23.13) or 'blind guides' (15.14; 23.16). Normally an epithet would represent an inadequate attempt on the part of one person to characterize another, inadequate because in life, as Bakhtin contends, we human beings react not to the whole of an individual but to those fragmentary parts of the individual's activity that are of special interest to us.[10] Therefore, even when we attempt to consider the whole of an individual, such as characterizing the individual as kind or vicious, these attempts do not truly represent an encompassing definition, but, according to Bakhtin, 'a prognosis of what we can and what we cannot expect from

10. Bakhtin, 'Author and Hero', 5.

him'.[11] Jesus, on the other hand, as we have seen, is no ordinary character. Like the author of a text with respect to his or her characters, Jesus is able to assemble all of the self-manifestations of the other characters: not only does Jesus know the thoughts of his opponents (9.4; 12.25),[12] he also knows their future, which is in principle unavailable to the conscious awareness of the other characters. For example, when Jesus finishes telling the parable of the vineyard, he declares to the chief priests and Pharisees that the kingdom of God will be taken from them and given to a nation producing the requisite fruit (21.43), a declaration that is implicitly fulfilled in Jesus' post-resurrection command to his disciples that they should make disciples of all the nations (28.19).

On the basis of Jesus' use of encompassing epithets, which in Matthew's Gospel are directed primarily against the Pharisees, it can be argued that the main opponents of Jesus are in fact the Pharisees. Although the extent of the correspondence between the narrative's character group the Pharisees and the principal historical opponents of Jesus and the church continues to be debated,[13] the prominence of the Pharisees in the narrative world of Matthew's Gospel is indisputable, as Garland, among others, has demonstrated on the basis of his synoptic comparison.[14] Garland's subsequent caution against isolating the Pharisees 'as the chief enemies in Matthew except as they are Jewish leaders, who form a united front against Jesus',[15] merely reinforces the argument that the individual traits of the Pharisees do not replace, but supplement, the characteristics of the larger group to which the Pharisees belong, namely, the Jewish leaders.

It is commonly accepted that the root trait of the Pharisees is hypocrisy. Even Kingsbury, who argues that the root trait of the Jewish leaders as a whole is 'evilness', concludes that they 'evince their evilness most prominently in the fact that they show themselves to be "hypocritical"'.[16] Kingsbury then proceeds to define hypocrisy as a type of 'inner incongruity'—

11. Bakhtin, 'Author and Hero', 5.

12. Similarly, Jesus is 'aware' of the Pharisees' plot to destroy him (12.14-15) and of the malice behind their question regarding the payment of taxes to Caesar (22.18).

13. For example, Davies and Allison, *Matthew*, I, 302, and Minear, *Matthew*, 11, argue in favor of correspondence. On the other hand, Sjef van Tilborg, *The Jewish Leaders in Matthew* (Leiden: E.J. Brill, 1972), 29, concludes that '[t]he Pharisees are not taken as a historical group by Mt, but as types of evil'.

14. David E. Garland, *The Intention of Matthew 23* (NovTSup, 52; Leiden: E.J. Brill, 1979), 45.

15. Garland, *Intention*, 221.

16. Kingsbury, *Matthew as Story*, 19.

the condition of being ' "divided" in one's fealty to God'.[17] This definition implies not only an awareness of God's demands, but also an intention to accomplish them. The condition of inner incongruity, however, which is characteristic of the hypocrite, also implies the presence of another intention, another compelling loyalty, which the hypocrite serves as well. The question is whether this condition of divided loyalties expresses itself primarily as conscious pretense or as a type of self-deception. In other words, do hypocrites intend to fool others or are they themselves deceived, such that they are not entirely aware of their own inner incongruity?

The importance of understanding the meaning of hypocrisy in Matthew's Gospel, in particular as the defining character trait of the Pharisees, is especially evident in the case of Bakhtin's model of reader–character interaction: in accordance with Bakhtin's model, the readers themselves are addressed as those whose inner incongruity belies their implicit claim to be disciples of the risen Lord. In other words, they are addressed as hypocrites, regardless of their own self-understanding.

Hypocrisy as the Defining Trait of the Pharisees

One of the problems of interpreting the meaning of hypocrisy in Matthew's Gospel, as Garland has observed, is the tendency to impose on Matthew's text a modern definition of hypocrisy, which understands the word 'in terms of pretending to be or representing oneself to be a better person than one really is'.[18] Although there is much evidence in Matthew's Gospel that hypocrisy should be understood as the discrepancy between appearance and reality, between the outside of a person and the inside, the charge of *conscious* pretense is actually more difficult to establish. Garland, for one, concludes that this sense of conscious dissimulation 'can only be considered as one aspect of its meaning',[19] as in the example of the Pharisees and Herodians confronting Jesus concerning the matter of paying taxes to Caesar (22.15-22): by conspiring to entrap Jesus, they are shown to be acting insincerely.[20] However, as Garland notes, it is not the insincerity of the Jewish leaders—their conscious pretense—that is emphasized in this scene, but rather their malice (*ponēria*), which Jesus recognizes, calling them 'hypocrites' (22.18). Indeed, their attempt to entrap

---

17. Kingsbury, *Matthew as Story*, 20.
18. Garland, *Intention*, 96.
19. Garland, *Intention*, 100.
20. Garland, *Intention*, 100-101 n. 29.

Jesus is in fact *consistent* with their inner conviction, which is a malevo-
lence toward Jesus. Therefore, Garland concludes that 'hypocrisy' for Matthew is similar to *ponēria*. Garland reaches a similar conclusion regarding
the meaning of hypocrisy in 6.2, 5, 16, where hypocrites are condemned
for intending their piety to be praised by others: '…there is no indication
that they were acting a part which contradicted their inner convictions;
they falsely believed that God would be as tickled with their manifesta-
tions of piety as men were.'[21] In other words, the hypocrites in the latter
examples are not primarily playing a conscious part, intending to deceive
others; rather, they themselves are deceived that their actions would be
acceptable to God.

Garland's conclusion that the dominant meaning of hypocrisy in Matthew's Gospel is a type of self-deception that represents a lack of self-
knowledge rather than the conscious deception of others, is cited with
approval by Dan Via.[22] Via, however, defines self-deception as more than
a lack of self-knowledge, although blindness is certainly a component of
self-deception. Rather, it is the paradoxical condition of 'really believing
but also not believing what is false'.[23] In other words, Via describes a condition of inner contradiction, a type of blindness for which the hypocrite is
nevertheless ultimately held responsible, at least in part:

> If the hypocrite is not consciously and cynically pretending, he is still
> responsible for being unconscious of the dichotomy between self-image and
> reality. The hypocrite may not intend to deceive others, but he does lack
> integrity, correspondence between inner and outer, and is responsible for
> the deficiency because he has concealed the true nature of the inner person
> from himself.[24]

To speak about concealing one's true nature from one's self, in other
words, is to point to an inner contradiction, in addition to the contradiction
between the outside of a person and the inside.

Inasmuch as Via's argument is based to a considerable extent on his
interpretation of the Matthean texts that refer to a contradiction between
the outside of a person and the inside, I shall begin my analysis of hypocrisy by examining the passages that establish correspondence—between
the inside of a person and the outside—as the norm of human existence,
namely, the metaphorical passages about the tree and its fruit.

21. Garland, *Intention*, 101 n. 29.
22. Via, *Self-Deception*, 93.
23. Via, *Self-Deception*, 93.
24. Via, *Self-Deception*, 94.

Tree and Fruit

Matthew affirms the principle that there exists a natural correspondence between the inside of a person and the outside, as evidenced by the evangelist's adaptation of the proverbial expression that a tree is known by its fruit (12.33): the immediate context of the metaphor describes the good/evil man who brings forth good/evil out of his good/evil treasure (12.35), an image that establishes the tree–fruit correspondence as a metaphor of human existence in general. The inside refers to a person's heart, which is the seat of human understanding and intention. Although Matthew does not link treasure and heart in 12.35, the connection is certain on the basis of the preceding verse: 'For out of the abundance of the heart the mouth speaks' (12.34). Furthermore, according to the same verse, when Matthew speaks about the fruit or outside of a person, he is referring to what a person says. Therefore, the correspondence between tree and fruit, that is, between the inside of a person and the outside, is a correspondence between heart and word, a correspondence that, in principle, is certain. Support for this interpretation comes from Matthew's warning that at the eschatological judgment one will be held accountable for 'every careless word' (12.36-37), a warning that confirms the principle that words reveal the heart.

Matthew affirms the same correspondence in principle between the inside of a person and the outside with respect to a person's deeds: Jesus warns the crowds and his disciples to beware of false prophets whose deeds will show them inwardly to be ravenous wolves, a correspondence that is expressed by the same tree–fruit metaphor (7.15-20). So certain is this correspondence that the criterion of eschatological judgment is defined solely in terms of one's deeds (25.31-46),[25] which implies that deeds are the adequate measure of one's heart or inner disposition. Although nothing is mentioned about words in the parable of the last judgment, one would expect that if words were able adequately to express the heart, then words should suffice as the criterion of judgment (cf. 12.36-37).

Apparently, however, words alone, even correct words, are not sufficient for entering the kingdom of heaven: some of those who call upon Jesus as Lord, performing mighty works in his name, will be excluded from the kingdom, because they did not do the will of God (7.21-23). But if words alone are not sufficient for entering the kingdom, then it is not

---

25. So Russell Pregeant, *Christology beyond Dogma: Matthew's Christ in Process Hermeneutic* (Semeia Supplements, 7; Philadelphia: Fortress Press; Missoula, MT: Scholars Press, 1978), 122-23.

true that words always reveal the heart, it is not true, with respect to words, that the tree is always known by its fruit. As a matter of fact, words can actually conceal the heart, as implied by Jesus' rhetorical question to the Pharisees: 'How can you speak good, when you are evil?' (12.34). Apparently, the Pharisees are capable of speaking correct words, despite having evil hearts. This interpretation is supported by Jesus' acknowledgment that the Pharisees sit on the chair of Moses (23.2), even though they are 'full of hypocrisy and iniquity' within (23.28).

The condition wherein words do not in fact reveal the heart represents not only a failure of the outside of a person to correspond to the inside, it contradicts the very principle of correspondence that Matthew affirms for both words and deeds. Therefore, if it is possible for words to conceal the heart, then it is possible for deeds to conceal the heart as well: when the false prophets testify before the judge that they prophesied in his name, cast out demons in his name, and performed mighty works in his name, all of which appear to be good deeds, they are nevertheless sent away as evil-doers who failed to do the will of God (7.21-23). Therefore, as Via concludes, it is impossible 'to know whether acts in any particular situation really reveal or conceal the heart'.[26] Inasmuch as God alone is able to see the true condition of the heart, all acts, even acts of apparent righteousness, are subject to the eschatological judgment, at which time it will be revealed whether the acts of righteousness proceeded from a good heart or an evil one, whether they were truly acts of righteousness or only apparently so.

Words and Deeds

Although it is impossible to know whether any particular word or deed conceals or reveals the heart, it is certain that correct words (12.37) and righteous deeds (16.27; 25.34-36) are necessary for salvation. The question is whether both are necessary for salvation, or whether eschatological justification is possible on the basis of either correct words or righteous deeds alone, so long as they correspond to a reconstituted heart. Daniel Patte, for one, has detected an apparent tension between Matthew's assertion that one is justified on the basis of words (12.37) and the earlier assertion, which constitutes the readers' understanding until this point in the narrative, that one is justified on the basis of deeds (7.21-23; 11.19).[27] Inasmuch as Matthew has shown himself to be a reliable author, so Patte contends, a resolution of this apparent tension is possible if one first limits

26. Via, *Self-Deception*, 92.
27. Patte, *Matthew*, 179.

the interpretation of the two tree–fruit passages (7.15-20; 12.33-37) to their immediate contexts.[28]

In the case of 7.15-20, the context is uncertain. Patte's division of verses links only 7.13-14 with 7.15-20; 7.21-27 is handled as a separate section.[29] Francis Beare broadens the context to include 7.13-27, but sees this section merely as the sermon on the mount's concluding series of exhortations and warnings.[30] David Hill also proposes a broader context, which is 7.13-29.[31] However, his suggestion that these final sayings are joined together by the common theme of warning fails to improve upon Beare's division: from Hill's discussion it is clear that he treats these as four separate sections. Günther Bornkamm, on the other hand, argues persuasively for the broader context on the basis of his conclusions regarding Jesus' verbatim repetition of the Baptist's proclamation that the kingdom of heaven is at hand (3.2 = 4.17).[32] Bornkamm sees in this shared message of repentance a clue that the evangelist intends for the Baptist to fill the role as a 'preacher of [Matthew's] congregation'.[33] From this observation follows an additional Baptist–Jesus comparison: as the Baptist rejects the Pharisees and Sadducees, who presume their salvation by virtue of their status (3.7-10), so also Jesus rejects false prophets (7.15-23), implicitly for the same reason.

When one reads the tree–fruit metaphor of 7.15-20 in terms of this broader context, it is clear that in this case the metaphor speaks of the necessity of good deeds that manifest a corresponding inner disposition.[34] Nevertheless, the good deeds themselves are set in the context of good words: those who do the will of the Father are among those who have spoken the correct words (7.21).[35] In other words, an interpretation of the tree–fruit metaphor of 7.15-20 is that good words (7.21) are expected to be

28. Patte, *Matthew*, 179.

29. Patte, *Matthew*, 98-101.

30. Francis Wright Beare, *The Gospel According to Matthew* (San Francisco: Harper & Row, 1981), 193-200.

31. David Hill, *The Gospel of Matthew* (New Century Bible Commentary; Grand Rapids: Eerdmans, 1972), 149-55.

32. Günther Bornkamm, 'End-Expectation and Church in Matthew', in Günther Bornkamm, Gerhard Barth and Heinz J. Held, *Tradition and Interpretation in Matthew* (Philadelphia: Westminster Press, 1963), 15-51 (15-17).

33. Bornkamm, 'End-Expectation', 15.

34. So Patte, *Matthew*, 179.

35. Patte, *Matthew*, 179.

matched by good deeds, which may (10.1, 8) or may not (7.22-23) include mighty works.

The context of the tree–fruit metaphor of 12.33-37, on the other hand, is clearly the preceding Beelzebul controversy (12.22-32).[36] Patte interprets this controversy as a portrayal of conflicting views of authority.[37] According to the Pharisaic conception of power and authority, which is implicit in this pericope, 'one has power only over those who recognize one's authority'.[38] Because Jesus manifests power over the demons, it follows that the demons must recognize his authority, which the Pharisees believe comes from Beelzebul himself. Clearly, from the perspective of the Gospel's dominant value system, these words of accusation against Jesus are not good words. Rather, they are the words for which the speakers will be condemned on the day of judgment (12.36-37).

In the light of Matthew's explicit statements elsewhere that righteous deeds are necessary for salvation (5.20; 6.14-15; 7.21-23; 16.27; 18.35; 25.31-46), the absence of any mention of deeds in the Beelzebul pericope seems surprising. Patte concludes, however, that the emphasis in 12.33-37 has been placed on good words as the precondition for doing good deeds.[39] In this instance, good words are the proper acknowledgment of Jesus' authority, the conviction that he casts out demons by the Spirit of God (12.28). But to speak of good words as the *acknowledgment* of Jesus' authority is ultimately to characterize the heart itself as good, affirming the principle of correspondence between heart and word. For it is the *view* of Jesus' authority, according to Patte, not merely correct words, that 'causes [the people] to bear good or bad fruit'.[40] Consequently, unless one is able to discern correctly the source of Jesus' power, that is, unless the heart as the seat of understanding and intention is properly constituted, one cannot perform truly good deeds. Nevertheless, as Patte argues, people are responsible for their deeds, whether good or bad, because, in the context of the Beelzebul controversy, they are personally responsible for their own view of the relationship between power and authority: 'They can choose to

36. So Patte, *Matthew*, 176-79; Beare, *The Gospel According to Matthew*, 275-81; Hill, *The Gospel of Matthew*, 216-19; and Davies and Allison, *Matthew*, II, 332, who define Mt. 12.22-37 as an extended objection story.

37. Patte, *Matthew*, 176-78.

38. Patte, *Matthew*, 176.

39. Patte, *Matthew*, 179.

40. Patte, *Matthew*, 178.

reject the view of religious authority and power that the Pharisees have; then they will be a good tree and bear good fruit.'[41]

If the Pharisees in Matthew's Gospel have the wrong view of Jesus' authority, making it impossible for them to perform truly good deeds, how then, as Jesus asks, can they still speak the good (12.34)? Patte's explanation is that they cannot; they only *apparently* speak the good: the Pharisees are those 'who appear to say good things while they are still evil, that is, while they still have the wrong view of religious authority'.[42] This interpretation is consistent with the view that righteous deeds may in fact be only apparently righteous, pending the eschatological judgment of the heart. There remains, however, an unresolved tension between this interpretation and Jesus' instructions elsewhere to practice what the Pharisees teach (23.2-3): implicitly, the teaching of the Pharisees in 23.2-3 is more than just the apparent good; it is indeed the good, even though it does not correspond to the heart.[43] Therefore, it must somehow be possible to speak the good while still being evil. Although one can ascribe this contradiction between the inside of a person and the outside to the condition of fallen humanity, as Via does,[44] a more complex view of the heart, a divided heart, which is itself an expression of fallen humanity, can also account for the data.

A Divided Heart

Kingsbury defines hypocrisy as 'a form of inner incongruity', wherein the single-minded, perfect devotion to God is lacking: 'To be perfect is to be wholehearted, or single-hearted, in the devotion with which one serves God (5.48; Deut. 18.13). To be hypocritical is to be "divided" in one's fealty to God.'[45] Although Kingsbury describes hypocrisy as an internal contradiction, the examples of hypocrisy that he cites refer to the contradiction between the inside of a person and the outside, or the contradiction between word and deed: 'paying honor to God with the lips while the heart is far from him (15.7-8); making pronouncements about what is right while not practicing them (23.3c); and appearing outwardly to be righteous

---

41. Patte, *Matthew*, 178.

42. Patte, *Matthew*, 179.

43. One is reminded of Paul's insistence that regardless of whether the gospel is proclaimed 'in pretense or in truth', it is nevertheless proclaimed, an outcome for which Paul rejoices (Phil. 1.15-18).

44. Via, *Self-Deception*, 79.

45. Kingsbury, *Matthew as Story*, 20.

while being inwardly full of lawlessness (23.28).[46] While these contradictions can ultimately be attributed to an inner incongruity, Kingsbury does not actually describe the phenomenon of a divided heart.

Via too recognizes the possibility that, under the condition of fallen existence, even the renewed heart of a believer might somehow be divided. For if the disciples, 'who have believed and seen the truth and who have had their hearts renewed', can still be characterized as having little faith (6.30; 8.26; 14.31; 16.8),[47] then the contradiction between the inside of a person and the outside cannot simply be ascribed to an evil heart. Rather, the failure of the disciples to manifest consistent faith implies that somehow 'the heart is both renewed and not renewed',[48] which itself is a serviceable definition of a divided heart. This condition of a divided heart explains, according to Via, how it is possible for a person to do better or worse than she is: the acts of a person 'may be better than the (unredeemed) heart (7.11) and worse than the (redeemed) heart (16.17-20, 23; 26.41)'.[49]

If, on the other hand, the contradiction between the inside of person and the outside can be reconceptualized as the manifestation of an inner contradiction, then it would be possible not only to explain the source of apparently good words and deeds but also to uphold the principle of correspondence between the tree and its fruit. Although in life the definitive characterization of words and deeds as good or evil cannot be established until the judgment, inasmuch as God alone can see the heart, the concept of a divided heart at least enables the readers of Matthew's Gospel to ascribe all words and deeds to their source, namely, the respective parts of a divided heart.

Jesus and the Pharisees

Bakhtin's 'model' of aesthetic contemplation is philosophically grounded in his understanding of self–other relations, which Bakhtin conceives as a productive relationship of two, noncoinciding perspectives. The perspective of the author/other is distinguished by its surplus of vision with respect to the hero/self, which surplus enables the author to enframe the whole of the hero within a consummating environment. The perspective of

46. Kingsbury, *Matthew as Story*, 20.
47. Via, *Self-Deception*, 82.
48. Via, *Self-Deception*, 82.
49. Via, *Self-Deception*, 82.

the hero/self, on the other hand, is characterized by the forward-directed-ness of the hero's inner life, which makes it impossible for the hero ever to achieve from within himself or herself a vantage point sufficient to encompass the whole of his or her own life. Nevertheless, the hero is still impelled to seek consummated images of himself or herself in the authoring vision of others.

This relationship between the open-ended perspective of the hero and the consummating perspective of the author was later reconceptualized by Bakhtin during his linguistic period as a relationship between one's own discourse and the discourse of others, whether the internally persuasive speech of others, which is affirmed and tightly woven to one's own discourse, or their authoritative speech, which is internalized but not as-similated by the self. Indeed, human consciousness itself comes to be understood by Bakhtin essentially as a type of inner dialogue, a 'process of selectively assimilating the words of others'.[50] One's own word, one's very apprehension of the world, 'is gradually and slowly wrought out of others' words that have been acknowledged and assimilated'.[51] Bakhtin's view of human consciousness as an inner dialogue of persuasive and authoritative voices commends itself as a means of conceptualizing the construct of a divided heart, the seat of human understanding and inten-tion. Inasmuch as the Pharisees, like the other Jewish leaders, are essentially cutouts who lack any character development in the course of the story,[52] the analysis of a single dialogic encounter between Jesus and the Pharisees is sufficient to establish the value of Bakhtin's approach. In order to demonstrate the validity of this hypothesis we must be able to find evidence of the struggle between competing voices in the perspective of the Pharisees. I propose that such evidence is available in the Beelzebul controversy (12.22-37), where the Pharisees are challenged by Jesus regarding the source of their (apparently) good words (12.34).

Matthew 12.22-37

As implied by the question of Jesus—'If I cast out demons by Beelzebul, by whom do your sons cast them out?' (12.27), the Pharisees have ascribed the works of their exorcist sons to the power of God. Therefore, it can be said that they have indeed 'spoken' good words. Moreover, they have spoken these good words even though they themselves are evil (12.34). In

---

50. Bakhtin, 'Discourse in the Novel', 341.
51. Bakhtin, 'Discourse in the Novel', 345 n. 31.
52. Kingsbury, *Matthew as Story*, 18.

other words, the Pharisees have spoken words, to paraphrase Via, that are better than their unredeemed heart. Such an interpretation is consistent with Matthew's assertion elsewhere that it is possible to speak good words even though one is evil at heart: judgment befalls those who speak good words (7.21; 23.2-3) but fail to do the will of God (7.21; 23.3). Nevertheless, despite these good words, the Pharisees are still condemned by Jesus, who characterizes the Pharisees as those who have uttered a 'careless word' (12.36).

According to Patte, the phrase 'careless word' refers in general to words uttered carelessly, but it refers especially to the blasphemous words spoken against the Spirit:[53] inasmuch as the charge of blasphemy against the Spirit (12.31-32) provides the occasion for this saying, it follows that such blasphemy is an example of the careless word for which the speaker will be held accountable (12.36-37). Yet what about other careless words? Words against the Son of man, for example, will be forgiven (12.32). Indeed, *every* other sin and blasphemy will be forgiven (12.31). Therefore, the expression 'careless word' probably does not refer merely to evil words; rather, it refers to inconsistent words, which inconsistency itself represents a type of failed correspondence, not unlike the condition wherein words fail to correspond to the heart.

In the Beelzebul controversy, the accusation of inconsistent speech apparently is leveled against the Pharisees for ascribing the same outcome (exorcism) to different sources (God and Beelzebul) simply because the exorcisms are performed by different agents (their sons and Jesus). While it is implied that the Pharisees have spoken the truth in the case of their sons, they have not done so in the case of Jesus. Therefore, Jesus rightly demands of them consistency. But if the Pharisees have spoken the truth in the case of their sons, it is because the Pharisees' words must correspond to a correct view of authority with respect to God: it is true that God casts out demons, in this instance, using the agency of their sons. On the other hand, the Pharisees are unable to see that God can cast out demons using the agency of Jesus, apparently because he scandalizes them (15.12). But if Jesus represents God's supreme agent in Matthew's Gospel, then one questions whether the Pharisees have truly appropriated their correct view of God, or whether, in Bakhtin's terminology, the authoritative word of Scripture has not remained for them a distant, unassimilated voice.

53. Patte, *Matthew*, 179.

The Divided Perspective of the Pharisees

The perspective of the Pharisees, when reconceptualized as Bakhtin's ideological consciousness, shows itself to be constituted by competing voices of authority and internal persuasiveness. The authoritative voice demands unconditional allegiance: it cannot be modified, and nor does it interact with other discourses; it can only be totally affirmed or totally rejected. The internally persuasive word, on the other hand, represents the creative appropriation of other discourses, a new voice that emerges out of the 'interanimating relationships with new contexts'.[54] An analysis of the Pharisees' perspective, or ideological consciousness, suggests that it comprises at least four voices, only one of which, it turns out, is internally persuasive for them: (1) the word of God; (2) the word of Jesus; (3) the tradition of the elders; and (4) the praise of men.

Word of God. The word of God is clearly authoritative for the Pharisees, indeed for all the Jewish leaders. When Jesus forgives the sins of the paralytic (9.2),[55] the scribes view his action as blasphemous (9.3), apparently believing, as Davies and Allison conclude, that 'Jesus has taken to himself a divine prerogative'.[56] Although the scribes' evaluation of Jesus' activity is incorrect from the perspective of the Gospel's dominant value system, it nevertheless implies that the word of God is authoritative for them: forgiveness of sins is indeed the prerogative of God. Subsequently, when the Pharisees see Jesus at table with tax collectors and sinners, they confront his disciples with Jesus' violation of the rules governing table fellowship (9.10-13). Although it is possible, as Patte argues, that the Pharisees consider Jesus' association with tax collectors and sinners to be a transgression of 'boundaries set by law, between what is pure and impure',[57] the matter of Jesus' purity is not in fact raised as an issue: indeed, in the sermon on the mount Jesus must forestall the more serious accusation that he came to abolish the law and the prophets (5.17). Rather, as the citation of Hos. 6.6 suggests, the presence of Jesus at table with sinners actualizes the forgiveness of their sins (9.13). Likewise, when the Pharisees observe the disciples plucking grain on the Sabbath, apparently

54. Bakhtin, 'Discourse in the Novel', 346.
55. As Davies and Allison, *Matthew*, II, 89, conclude, Jesus is not merely declaring God's forgiveness, despite the possible presence of a divine passive, inasmuch as 9.6 'clearly states that the Son of man has authority to forgive sins'.
56. Davies and Allison, *Matthew*, II, 91.
57. Patte, *Matthew*, 129-30.

violating the prohibition against Sabbath work (12.2), Jesus, repeating his citation of Hos. 6.6, declares the law-breakers to be guiltless (12.7), because they are associated with him, the Lord of the Sabbath (12.8). Consequently, the Pharisees see in Jesus one who not only condones lawlessness but also has assumed the divine prerogative to forgive sins.

Word of Jesus. The authoritative word of God demands of the Pharisees their unconditional allegiance. Therefore, when the Pharisees witness Jesus, a friend of tax collectors and sinners, casting out demons, rather than reconsidering their view of Jesus, they accuse him of colluding with Beelzebul (12.24). When Jesus points out the contradiction of their perspective, reminding the Pharisees of their positive evaluation of their exorcist sons (12.27), he gives them the opportunity to recontextualize the word of God in the light of this new information. In other words, Jesus gives the Pharisees the opportunity to *assimilate* the authoritative word of God, to make it internally persuasive for themselves, by reconsidering their view of Jesus and his activity. The refusal of the Pharisees to assimilate this word of Jesus, however, demonstrates the ultimate unfruitfulness of God's word for them: it remains merely an authoritative word.

Jesus, on the other hand, *is* able to assimilate and recontextualize the word of God, demonstrating that God's word is internally persuasive for him: in response to the Pharisees' accusation that his work of healing violates the prohibition against work on the Sabbath, Jesus declares that 'it is lawful to do good on the sabbath' (12.12). Moreover, this word of Jesus is itself presented as an authoritative word (cf. 7.28); it demands total acceptance or total rejection, as evidenced by Jesus' warning to the Pharisees: 'He who is not with me is against me, and he who does not gather with me scatters' (12.30). The uncompromising nature of Jesus' word is confirmed by his insistence that his disciples must place allegiance to him above even their familial obligations (4.22; 8.22; 10.37). Consequently, the Pharisees, who are unable to comprehend that Scripture itself might only be, in Via's words, 'a possible clue to the will of God, a trace left on Israel's religious culture by the will of God',[58] totally reject Jesus' authoritative word (12.14), believing thereby that they are doing God's will.

Tradition of Elders. Although the Pharisees have implicitly endorsed the view that their sons cast out demons by the Spirit of God, a recontextualization characteristic of internally persuasive speech, the Pharisees'

---

58. Via, *Self-Deception*, 88.

inability to acknowledge the authority of Jesus implies instead that their view of the exorcist sons represents for them yet another unassimilated, authoritative word, albeit an interpreted word, a kind of tradition of the elders. Inasmuch as allegiance to the tradition of the elders is characteristic of the Pharisees (15.2), it seems reasonable to infer that the tradition has indeed accredited the exorcist sons. The Pharisees' unshakable allegiance to the tradition of the elders indicates that the tradition functions for the Pharisees remarkably like the authoritative word of God: not only are they anxious when others, such as the disciples of Jesus, do not honor their hand-washing tradition (15.2), they themselves risk transgression of the commandments of God for the sake of their traditions (15.3-6). Perhaps at one time, in the time of the elders, the positive appraisal of the exorcist sons represented a reaccentuated, internally persuasive word; for the Pharisees, however, it is simply a distant, authoritative word demanding of them their unconditional allegiance.

Praise of Men. Despite the failure of the Pharisees to recontextualize these expressions of authoritative discourse with respect to the matter of Jesus' exorcisms, the Pharisees nevertheless have managed to reaccentuate the authoritative voices in their dealings with the people: the word of God and the tradition of the elders become the means by which the Pharisees secure the praise of men. When Jesus warns his followers not to practice their piety 'before men in order to be seen by them' (6.1), although the Pharisees are not mentioned by name, Jesus' use of the epithet 'hypocrites' (6.2, 5, 16; cf. 23.13, 15, 23, 25, 27, 29) implies that he has the Pharisees (and scribes) in mind. Therefore, the warning of Jesus, who knows their inner thoughts, characterizes the Pharisees as those who practice a piety that is motivated by the desire for human praise, even though the explicit intention of the piety is to please God.

Inasmuch as the word of God, which is authoritative for the Pharisees, commends almsgiving, in order for that word to be internally persuasive for the Pharisees, they must recontextualize the requirement of the law in their own lives. When Jesus teaches his followers how to practice their piety, by giving alms in secret (6.3-4), praying in secret (6.6) and fasting in secret (6.17-18), he establishes the principle that authoritative words can indeed be recontextualized as internally persuasive ones such that the intention of the law is fulfilled, thus achieving the coincidence of authority and internal persuasiveness in one word.

The Pharisees, however, recontextualize the demand of the law such that their own interests are served instead of God's. Not only, as Jesus' own authoritative word asserts, do the Pharisees seek the praise of men (6.2; cf. 6.1, 5, 16), their desire for praise actually becomes a heavy burden laid upon the shoulders of others (23.4).[59] Although most scholars interpret the 'heavy burdens' of 23.4 as referring to the multiplied burdens of the Pharisaic interpretation of the law,[60] which they could otherwise remove, when this verse is read in the context of the following verses, which speak of deeds performed 'to be seen by men' (23.5-7), it is possible to understand it as yet another reference to seeking the praise of men. It is generally acknowledged that 23.4 is best read in terms of 11.28, where Jesus invites others to accept his yoke, the light burden. As Gundry points out, however, the lightness of Jesus' burden does not consist of 'any laxity in Jesus' teaching (much to the contrary, see 5.17-48!), but with his meekness and humility, which contrast sharply with the scribes' and Pharisees' overweening desire for recognition'.[61] In other words, it is the praise of men, rather than the word of God, that is internally persuasive for the Pharisees.

This internally persuasive word of the Pharisees, their creative appropriation of another's discourse, is in a sense hidden from them: the Pharisees would claim that they are doing the will of God. Only the intervention of Jesus, who knows both their thoughts and their end, is able to bring to light the Pharisees' failure to appropriate the word of God correctly. However, rather than assimilating the word of Jesus, a word that offers them insight, the Pharisees reject it, thus sealing their fate as plants destined to be uprooted (15.13), as blind guides who will fall into a pit (15.14).

The Reader's Appropriation of the Pharisees' Perspective

The reader of aesthetic contemplation, on the other hand, despite having momentarily accepted the limited perspective of the Pharisees, thus seeing Jesus in his veiled ordinariness as an agent of Beelzebul (9.34; 12.24) and a condoner of lawlessness (9.10-11; 12.1-2; 15.1-2), nevertheless also understands more than the Pharisees: the reader of aesthetic contemplation also knows that Jesus is indeed God's supreme agent (28.18), whose word for the Pharisees is not only a word of judgment but at the same time a word that is able to reconstitute a divided heart. Like the Pharisees, who

59. So Gundry, *Matthew*, 455-56.

60. So H. Benedict Green, *The Gospel According to Matthew* (New Clarendon Bible; London: Oxford University Press, 1975), 189; Garland, *Intention*, 50-51; Patte, *Matthew*, 321-22.

61. Gundry, *Matthew*, 456.

seek to appropriate God's authoritative word, the readers are confronted with the same problem of assimilating the authoritative word of Jesus, which, according to Bakhtin, resists assimilation and recontextualization, demanding instead unconditional allegiance. Therefore, in order for the word of Jesus to become an internally persuasive word for the readers, they must first come to recognize that their anxiety before the veil of Jesus' ordinariness represents a failure to assimilate his word correctly, which failure is the same as that of the Pharisees, who misappropriate the authoritative word of God. Unlike the Pharisees, on the other hand, the reader of aesthetic contemplation potentially is able to be 'authored' by Jesus, who is both the carpenter's son and God's supreme agent, which encounter exposes the reader's little faith for what it really is—the equivalence of the unbelief of the Pharisees, who seek the death of Jesus (12.14).

For the readers to be so authored by Jesus is to be cast out of the character group the disciples, whereupon the readers find themselves in the same condition of potentiality as the outsider supplicants, once again awaiting the granting of divine forgiveness and the eschatological knowledge of the law.

Chapter 7

CONCLUSION

Not the Righteous but Sinners

It has been argued that the concluding aphorism of the parable of the wedding feast—'For many are called but few are chosen' (22.14)—should be understood in a Semitic sense: 'All are called but not all are chosen.'[1] The indiscriminate nature of the call, which is evident in the repeated summons of the parable, the final summons being a command to bring everyone to the feast regardless of his or her status, is reminiscent of the liberal sowing of the seed in the parable of the sower: seed falls along the path, on rocky ground, among thorns, as well as on good soil (13.3-8). These metaphors of the messianic invitation appear to stand in tension with the more restrictive words of Jesus in the table scene: 'For I came not to call the righteous, but sinners' (9.13). The apparently more restrictive words, however, need not be understood as contradicting the indiscriminate invitation, if one attends closely to the roles of the major character groups as they are presented in the Gospel's narrative world. Inasmuch as the ultimate addressees of these narrative scenes are the readers of Matthew's Gospel, who, as it is presupposed by this study, are already familiar with Matthew's narrative and endorse its values, all of the characters, regardless of their group membership, serve the same purpose: to reshape the readers' understanding, not simply by conveying discipleship values, but by reconstituting their heart, the very seat of their understanding and intention.

Although the restrictive words of Jesus explicitly exclude the righteous, the interactions between Jesus and the Pharisees, whether in the table scene or elsewhere in Matthew's Gospel, make it clear that these so-called righteous Pharisees are as much in need of Jesus' salvation as are the sinners for whom he avowedly comes. Unlike the sinners, however, whose

1. Davies and Allison, *Matthew*, III, 207.

supplication implies the recognition of their need, the Pharisees are unable to realize that they are in fact no better off than the sinners: the words of Jesus to the Pharisees do not elicit a penitential response on the part of the Pharisees; rather his words provoke the Pharisees to seek to destroy him (12.14).

While it might be argued that the words of Jesus to the Pharisees function as an indirect invitation, their failure to reconsider their status as the righteous suggests that Matthew's portrayal of the Pharisees' interaction with Jesus is not intended to depict a call, even an indirect one, but to warn others regarding the possibility of stubborn blindness. The absence of an understanding response on the part of the disciples (15.12), however, the principal narrative recipients of Jesus' teaching, suggests that Matthew depicts Jesus' confrontations with the Pharisees, not in order to warn other *characters* regarding the possibility of stubborn blindness, but to warn *the readers of Matthew's Gospel*, his ultimate addressees. Garland is certainly correct when he concludes that the purpose of the entire discourse of Mt. 23 is to warn the Church, even though the immediate addressees of 23.13-39 are the scribes and Pharisees, rather than the disciples.[2] To warn the readers of Matthew's Gospel about the possibility of stubborn blindness, however, is in a sense to characterize the readers themselves as conditioned by a type of blindness, in this case, a believer's blindness. In other words, it can be argued that the readers are not simply warned; they themselves are implicitly characterized by the text as those who do not recognize their true condition, which resembles that of the opponents of Jesus, who resist his call and seek his death. Therefore, a plausible interpretation of the more restrictive words of Jesus—that he came not to call the righteous—is that the recognition of need on the part of Matthew's readers is as necessary a condition for actualizing the messianic invitation as it is for the Pharisees, the principal opponents of Jesus in the narrative. For just as it can be said that Jesus did not come to call those who do not recognize their need, so also can it be said that Matthew's Gospel only calls those who acknowledge their need, who recognize that they are in fact sinners.

Who are the sinners in Matthew's Gospel? Certainly they are the tax collectors and sinners who sit at table with Jesus (9.10-13; 11.19). They

---

2.   Garland, *Reading Matthew*, 229. See also Via, *Self-Deception*, 92, who argues that Matthew's portrayal of the human condition makes it impossible to know whether acts reveal or conceal the heart, despite the evangelist's apparent claim to the contrary (7.16). Consequently, the warning to beware of false prophets (7.15) is turned against the reader: 'Beware of the false prophet in you.'

are also the supplicants, whose infirmity (9.2) or ethnic status (5.47; 6.7; 18.17) implies their sin. At first glance, those who are explicitly called by Jesus in the Gospel's narrative world—the disciples (4.18-22; 9.9)—also appear to fit the description of the sinners for whom Jesus comes: they are called from Galilee (4.18), the land of those who sit in darkness (4.15-16); they are among those who are characterized by Jesus as being evil (7.11); one of them is even a tax collector (9.9), a thoroughly negative epithet in Matthew's narrative world (5.46; 11.19; 18.17). However, although there is indeed some evidence that the disciples are sinners, such a description is not the foremost trait of their characterization. In the first place, when the disciples pluck grain on the Sabbath (12.1-8), in violation of an apparent Sabbath prohibition, Jesus nevertheless declares them to be guiltless (12.7). Secondly, by questioning the disciples about Jesus' fellowship in the table scene, the Pharisees implicitly acknowledge that they do not consider the disciples to be members of the character group the tax collectors and sinners. This suggests that the Gospel's characterization of the disciples is intended to emphasize for the readers a different trait than that of the tax collectors and sinners.

The conflicting interpretations of the status of the disciples in the grainfields pericope suggest that the characterization 'sinner' can be seen in a different light, depending on how one defines the roles of the character groups with respect to their proximity to the Jewish leadership and Jesus—the narrative's principal centers of authority. In the grainfields pericope the disciples are pronounced guiltless of violating the Sabbath simply because they are with Jesus (12.1-8), which relationship is said to be constitutive of Matthean discipleship (18.20; 28.20). Inasmuch as the disciples are portrayed primarily as those who are with Jesus, their sin is defined by Jesus (5.21-48; 15.17-20; 18.5-9), rather than by the Jewish leadership. The sinners, on the other hand, who represent the marginal members of Jewish religious society, are never depicted as becoming members of the character group the disciples. Therefore, their sin is defined by the Jewish religious elite.

Although the recognition of sin implicitly constitutes the self-understanding of the sinners, it is noteworthy that sin itself does not appear to be the foremost trait of their characterization: only the disciples are actually charged by the Pharisees with transgressing the law (12.2) or the tradition of the elders (15.2). Rather, the foremost trait of the sinners is their status as the Gospel's consummate outsiders, marginalized by the Jewish religious elite yet never actually portrayed as members of the character group the disciples despite the fruitful reception of the messianic invitation by the supplicants, the paradigmatic members of their character group. As outsiders, the supplicants, in particular the Gentile supplicants, function as threshold characters, as McCracken would say,[3] whose sole purpose is to bring the readers to the threshold of the characters' decision, at which point in the narrative they are subsequently abandoned. The resolution of the supplicants' decision is depicted as the acceptance of their outsider's status, which represents a type of emptiness that establishes the possibility of being filled, as Via might argue.[4]

Unlike the supplicants, whose brief story leaves the readers at the threshold of the supplicants' decision, the disciples, in their capacity as those who are with Jesus, engage the readers in a long story that is essentially commensurate with the public ministry of Jesus, which foreshadows the arduous, ongoing life of discipleship (10.16-25; 24.9-14). Despite the assurance of Jesus' presence, however, the disciples are characterized as those of little faith (8.26; 17.20), as those who ultimately are unable to grasp the nature of Jesus' authority (20.25-28; 28.17). Therefore, rather than embodying the teaching of Jesus, who exhorts them not to be anxious (6.25-32; 10.19-33), they succumb to their anxiety, thereby expressing the failure of the metaphorical seed, which proves unfruitful in the face of persecution (13.21) and worldly cares (13.22). In other words, the disciples are possessed of a divided heart, the very condition of the Pharisees, the principal opponents of Jesus. Consequently, the failure of the disciples to manifest the faith of the supplicants represents the paradigmatic sin of those who are with Jesus, a type of unbelief within the community of believers, as Held has argued,[5] an unbelief that is the equivalence of the death-seeking posture of the Pharisees.[6]

Reader–Character Interaction in Matthew's Gospel

The readers' perception of role equivalence, while not limiting the narrative's rhetorical effects to those involving the character group the disciples, nevertheless potentially establishes the readers themselves as imperfect followers. This is because the mixed portrayal of the disciples does not

---

3.   McCracken, 'Character in the Boundary', 31-33.
4.   On emptiness as potentiality, see Via, *Self-Deception*, 123-27.
5.   Held, 'Miracle Stories', 294.
6.   See Heb. 6.4-6, where the author asserts that apostasy is the functional equivalence of crucifying the Son of God.

merely imply discipleship shortcomings on the part of Matthew's historical readers, nor does it simply warn against the possibility of discipleship shortcomings in general; it actually addresses all readers of Matthew's Gospel as imperfect disciples *in fact*, regardless of their own self-understanding. Therefore, unless the readers come to understand that they are imperfect disciples, then the Gospel, although addressed to them, will not be welcomed by them as the good news that is able to reconstitute a divided heart. Only a methodology that does not reject out of hand the negative character traits that are encountered during the process of the readers' interaction with the narrative's major character groups, however, encourages the readers to come to this realization.

The mechanism of a reading approach that momentarily accepts the negative traits of the character groups is by no means self-evident. Indeed, such a mechanism is at odds with prevailing contemporary theory, which, as we have seen, advocates a type of reader–character interaction intended to encourage the readers to accept the values of the Gospel's positive characters, such as the supplicants, and to reject those of the negative characters, such as the Pharisees. It has been my contention, however, that only by means of a Bakhtinian strategy of reader–character interaction are the readers, who already claim to endorse the values of the Gospel, truly engaged as Matthew's addressees. For it is by encouraging the readers to identify with the narrative opponents of Jesus in particular—or to recognize that they are in fact like the opponents, who resist his call and seek his death—that the Gospel is able to constitute the readers as sinners, thereby establishing them as the potential recipients of good news.

The unique characterization of Jesus, God's supreme agent who not only manifests God's values but also encompasses the limited perspective of the other characters, suggests an alternative to the reading strategies that encourage the emulation of Jesus' ethical behavior. Inasmuch as Jesus is portrayed as an 'aestheticized' absolute consciousness, the readers are precluded, according to the principles of aesthetic contemplation, from approaching him directly: apart from those aspects of his characterization that are necessary for any type of character portrayal, the readers are unable to find a stable position that is entirely outside the consciousness of Jesus. Without this stable position of outsideness with respect to Jesus, the readers cannot completely assemble the self-manifestations of Jesus into a unitary whole of meaning. The interaction between Jesus and the other characters of Matthew's Gospel, on the other hand, does offer the readers an approach to Jesus—through the agency of the narrative's other charac-

ters, all of whom can be aesthetically contemplated. The readers' identification with the various character groups, it has been argued, serves the
purpose of momentarily accepting not only the characters' values but more
importantly their limited perspective, which expresses itself primarily as a
limitation upon their knowledge with respect to the narrative's temporal
axis. Consequently, when the readers interact with Jesus, they must do so
through the veil of his ordinariness, momentarily without the benefit of the
post-resurrection declaration that all authority has been granted to him. For
the readers to approach Jesus through the agency of the other characters,
however, is at the same time to be 'authored' by the encompassing consciousness of God's supreme agent: in their capacity as co-authors, the
readers also know what the characters themselves cannot know—that
Jesus is indeed the one to whom all authority has been given (28.18),
whose word is able to reconstitute the readers' heart.

The Gentile supplicants in Matthew's Gospel are said to be paradigmatic for Matthew's readers, because they manifest great faith. Yet it
seems clear that their great faith is related to their recognition of need, a
type of emptiness that represents the condition of potentiality to be filled.
Although the recognition of need serves as the precondition for the
actualization of potentiality, it is also clear that it is the word of Jesus that
enables the supplicants to recognize their need in the first place: the
circulating word about Jesus initially brings the supplicants to Jesus (4.23-
25), while his subsequent word evokes their paradigmatic faith response
(8.7-10; 15.26-28). Arguably, therefore, in order for the readers to actualize the potentiality of need, they must find themselves in the same condition as the supplicants, a condition of need that cannot simply be
imitated. For the readers of Matthew's Gospel, this means not only that the
Gospel itself must ultimately fill their need, it must also create the
condition of need in the first place. Otherwise, like the disciples, who fail
to actualize the pattern of Jesus' life despite repeatedly hearing his
teaching, the readers will never become the fruitful receivers of his word.

It has been the argument of this study that Matthew's Gospel establishes
the readers in the condition of need by casting them in the role of the
Pharisees, who are unable to see through the veil of Jesus' scandalous
ordinariness, instead seeing in him an agent of Beelzebul (9.34; 12.24) and
a condoner of lawlessness (9.10-11; 12.1-2; 15.1-2). Nevertheless, the
readers' surplus of knowledge with respect to the Pharisees means that the
readers, unlike the Pharisees, are able to recognize that the one who addresses them is indeed God's supreme agent, whose word is also avowedly

authoritative for them. In other words, unlike the Pharisees, the readers are able to be 'authored' by Jesus, which encounter exposes the little faith of the disciples for what it really is—the unbelief of the Pharisees, who seek Jesus' death (12.14). For the readers to be so authored by Jesus is to be cast out of the character group the disciples, whereupon the readers find themselves in the same condition of potentiality as the outsider supplicants, once again awaiting the granting of divine forgiveness and the eschatological knowledge of the law. For in the ongoing life of discipleship, the readers must repeatedly come to recognize themselves as empty in order that the kingdom's presence might serve as the new potentiality for further actualization in the future. Otherwise, fullness will have the unintended effect of preventing the readers from seeing that they are in fact, this side of the eschaton, still empty.

Epilogue

When gospel critics study the interaction of the readers and Matthew's characters, they tend to reach similar conclusions, despite using different methodologies. The alternative reading that I have proposed is not intended as a refutation of the apparent scholarly consensus. To a great extent interpretive conclusions are dependent upon one's choice of methodology. The fact that gospel critics have reached similar conclusions regarding reader–character interaction, despite using different methodologies, may indicate that they have achieved an assured result. On the other hand, it may simply mean that their methodologies in fact are not appreciably different.

Interpretive conclusions are also dependent, of course, upon the type of questions that one asks of the text. Inasmuch as one of the main presuppositions of this study has been that the readers of Matthew's Gospel are rereaders, those who are already familiar with the narrative's values and rhetorical strategy, the principal question of this study has been, If the readers already endorse the values of Matthew's Gospel, what purpose do subsequent rereadings serve? Essentially, the answer has been that the Gospel establishes the readers as the potential recipients of good news, the narrative role of the supplicants, by addressing them as the potential opponents of the Gospel, the narrative role of the Pharisees.

The role of the readers, which Bakhtin understands as a type of secondary authoring, is to encounter Jesus of Nazareth through his interactions with the narrative's other characters, which interactions place the readers in the position of holding together the limited perspective of the characters and the fuller perspective of the readers' surplus, which they share with the author of Matthew's Gospel. The expected outcome of this reading strategy is that the readers, who confess Jesus of Nazareth to be the risen Lord, will also be forced to co-experience the limited perspective of the narrative's major character groups, each of which is confronted with the veil of Jesus' ordinariness. The explanation of the varied responses of the character groups—rejection, unfruitful reception and fruitful reception—is to be found in the characters' interactions with Jesus. However, the readers' activity of co-authoring these character interactions, as the activity is conceptualized by this study, is not intended so much to discover the explanation of the characters' responses as it is to present the readers themselves with the one who is able to reconstitute an unredeemed heart. This encounter is possible because the readers not only co-experience the limited perspective of the narrative's characters, but they do so in a way that the characters themselves cannot—they know that Jesus is the risen Lord, to whom all authority has been granted. Subsequently, in accordance with Bakhtin's project, the readers are expected to answer with their own lives for what they have learned in their encounter with Jesus of Nazareth, for what they have experienced and understood in the art of Matthew's Gospel.

BIBLIOGRAPHY

Adam, A.K.M., 'Matthew's Readers, Ideology, and Power', in E.H. Lovering Jr (ed.), *Society of Biblical Literature 1994 Seminar Papers* (Atlanta: Scholars Press, 1994), 435-49.

Albright, William Foxwell, and C.S. Mann, *Matthew* (AB, 26; Garden City: Doubleday, 1971).

Allen, Willoughby C., *A Critical and Exegetical Commentary on the Gospel According to St Matthew* (ICC; New York: Charles Scribner's Sons, 1907).

Allison, Dale C., Jr, *The New Moses: A Matthean Typology* (Philadelphia: Fortress Press, 1993).

Anderson, Janice Capel, 'Matthew: Gender and Reading', *Semeia* 28 (1983), 3-27.

—'Double and Triple Stories, the Implied Reader, and Redundancy in Matthew', *Semeia* 31 (1985), 71-89.

—*Matthew's Narrative Web: Over, and Over, and Over Again* (JSNTSup, 91; Sheffield: JSOT Press, 1994).

—'Life on the Mississippi: New Currents in Matthean Scholarship, 1983–1993', *Currents in Research: Biblical Studies* 3 (1995), 169-218.

Bacon, Benjamin W., *Studies in Matthew* (New York: Henry Holt, 1930).

Bakhtin, M.M., 'Discourse in the Novel', in Michael Holquist (ed.), *The Dialogic Imagination: Four Essays by M.M. Bakhtin* (trans. Caryl Emerson and Michael Holquist; Austin: University of Texas Press, 1981), 259-422.

—*Problems of Dostoevsky's Poetics* (ed. and trans. Caryl Emerson; Minneapolis: University of Minnesota Press, 1984).

—'The Problem of Speech Genres', in Emerson and Holquist (eds.), *Speech Genres*, 60-102.

—'The Problem of the Text in Linguistics, Philology, and the Human Sciences: An Experiment in Philosophical Analysis', in Emerson and Holquist (eds.), *Speech Genres*, 103-31.

—'Toward a Methodology for the Human Sciences', in Emerson and Holquist (eds.), *Speech Genres*, 159-72.

—'Art and Answerability', in Holquist and Liapunov (eds.), *Art and Answerability*, 1-3.

—'Author and Hero in Aesthetic Activity', in Holquist and Liapunov (eds.), *Art and Answerability*, 4-256.

Barth, Gerhard, 'Matthew's Understanding of the Law', in Bornkamm, Barth and Held, *Tradition and Interpretation in Matthew*, 58-164.

Bauer, David R., *The Structure of Matthew's Gospel: A Study in Literary Design* (JSNTSup, 31; Sheffield: Almond Press, 1988).

—'The Major Characters of Matthew's Story: Their Function and Significance', *Int* 46 (1992), 357-67.

Beare, Francis Wright, *The Gospel According to Matthew* (San Francisco: Harper & Row, 1981).

Beck, David R., 'The Narrative Function of Anonymity in Fourth Gospel Characterization', *Semeia* 63 (1993), 143-58.

Booth, Wayne C., *The Rhetoric of Fiction* (Chicago: University of Chicago Press, 1961).

Bornkamm, Günther, Gerhard Barth and Heinz J. Held, *Tradition and Interpretation in Matthew* (trans. Percy Scott; Philadelphia: Westminster Press, 1963).

Bornkamm, Günther, 'End-Expectation and Church in Matthew', in Bornkamm, Barth and Held, *Tradition and Interpretation in Matthew*, 15-51.

—'The Stilling of the Storm in Matthew', in Bornkamm, Barth and Held, *Tradition and Interpretation in Matthew*, 52-57.

Burnett, Fred W., 'Characterization in Matthew: Reader Construction of the Disciple Peter', *McKendree Pastoral Review* 4 (1987), 13-44.

—'Characterization and Reader Construction of Character in the Gospels', *Semeia* 63 (1993), 3-28.

Carter, Warren, 'The Crowds in Matthew's Gospel', *CBQ* 55 (1993), 54-67.

—*Households and Discipleship: A Study of Matthew 19-20* (JSNTSup, 103; Sheffield: JSOT Press, 1994).

—*Matthew: Storyteller, Interpreter, Evangelist* (Peabody, MA: Hendrickson, 1996).

—'Matthew 4.18-22 and Matthean Discipleship: An Audience-Oriented Perspective', *CBQ* 59 (1997): 58-75.

—'Jesus' "I Have Come" Statements in Matthew's Gospel', *CBQ* 60 (1998), 44-62.

Chatman, Seymour, *Story and Discourse: Narrative Structure in Fiction and Film* (Ithaca, NY: Cornell University Press, 1978).

Clark, Katerina, and Michael Holquist, *Mikhail Bakhtin* (Cambridge, MA: Harvard University Press, 1984).

Combrink, H.J. Bernard, 'The Structure of the Gospel of Matthew as Narrative', *TynBul* 34 (1983), 61-90.

Culpepper, R. Alan, *Anatomy of the Fourth Gospel: A Study in Literary Design* (Philadelphia: Fortress Press, 1983).

Darr, John A., *On Character Building: The Reader and the Rhetoric of Characterization in Luke–Acts* (Louisville,KY: Westminster/John Knox Press, 1992).

Davies, W.D., and Dale C. Allison Jr, *A Critical and Exegetical Commentary on the Gospel According to Saint Matthew* (ICC; 3 vols.; Edinburgh: T. & T. Clark, 1988–97).

Deutsch, Celia, *Hidden Wisdom and the Easy Yoke: Wisdom, Torah and Discipleship in Matthew 11.25-30* (JSNTSup, 18; Sheffield: JSOT Press, 1987).

Donaldson, Terence L., *Jesus on the Mountain: A Study in Matthean Theology* (JSNTSup, 8; Sheffield: JSOT Press, 1985).

Edwards, Richard A., *Matthew's Story of Jesus* (Philadelphia: Fortress Press, 1985).

—'Uncertain Faith: Matthew's Portrait of the Disciples', in Fernando F. Segovia (ed.), *Discipleship in the New Testament* (Philadelphia: Fortress Press, 1985), 47-61.

—*Matthew's Narrative Portrait of Disciples: How the Text-Connoted Reader Is Informed* (Harrisburg, PA: Trinity Press International, 1997).

Ellis, Peter F., *Matthew: His Mind and his Message* (Collegeville, MN: Liturgical Press, 1974).

Emerson, Caryl, and Michael Holquist (eds.), *Speech Genres and Other Late Essays* (trans. Vern W. McGee; Austin: University of Texas Press, 1986).

Fowler, Robert M., *Loaves and Fishes: The Function of the Feeding Stories in the Gospel of Mark* (Chico, CA: Scholars Press, 1981).

Garland, David E., *The Intention of Matthew 23* (NovTSup, 52; Leiden: E.J. Brill, 1979).

—*Reading Matthew: A Literary and Theological Commentary on the First Gospel* (New York: Crossroad, 1993).

Gerhardsson, Birger, *The Mighty Acts of Jesus According to Matthew* (trans. Robert Dewsnap; Lund: C.W.K. Gleerup, 1979).

Goulder, M.D., *Midrash and Lection in Matthew* (London: SPCK, 1974).

Green, Barbara, *Mikhail Bakhtin and Biblical Scholarship: An Introduction* (SBLSS; Atlanta: Society of Biblical Literature, 2000).

Green, H. Benedict, *The Gospel According to Matthew* (New Clarendon Bible; London: Oxford University Press, 1975).

Guelich, Robert A., *The Sermon on the Mount: A Foundation for Understanding* (Waco, TX: Word Books, 1982).

Gundry, Robert H., *Matthew: A Commentary on his Literary and Theological Art* (Grand Rapids: Eerdmans, 1982).

—'A Responsive Evaluation of the Social History of the Matthean Community in Roman Syria', in David L. Balch (ed.), *The Social History of the Matthean Community: Cross-Disciplinary Approaches* (Philadelphia: Fortress Press, 1991), 62-67.

Held, Heinz J., 'Matthew as Interpreter of the Miracle Stories', in Bornkamm, Barth and Held, *Tradition and Interpretation in Matthew*, 165-299.

Hill, David, *The Gospel of Matthew* (New Century Bible Commentary; Grand Rapids: Eerdmans, 1972).

—'On the Use and Meaning of Hosea VI.6 in Matthew's Gospel', *NTS* 24 (1977), 107-19.

—'The Figure of Jesus in Matthew's Story: A Response to Professor Kingsbury's Literary-Critical Probe', *JSNT* 21 (1984), 37-52.

Holquist, Michael, and Vadim Liapunov (eds.), *Art and Answerability: Early Philosophical Essays by M.M. Bakhtin* (trans. Vadim Liapunov; supplement trans. Kenneth Brostrom; Austin: University of Texas Press, 1990).

Holquist, Michael, 'Introduction: The Architectonics of Answerability', in Holquist and Liapunov (eds.), *Art and Answerability*, ix-xlix.

Holub, Robert C., *Reception Theory: A Critical Introduction* (London: Methuen, 1984).

Howell, David B., *Matthew's Inclusive Story: A Study in the Narrative Rhetoric of the First Gospel* (JSNTSup, 42; Sheffield: JSOT Press, 1990).

Iser, Wolfgang, *The Act of Reading: A Theory of Aesthetic Response* (Baltimore: The Johns Hopkins University Press, 1978).

Jefferson, Ann, 'Bodymatters: Self and Other in Bakhtin, Sartre and Barthes', in Ken Hirschkop and David Shepherd (eds), *Bakhtin and Cultural Theory* (Manchester: Manchester University Press, 1989), 152-77.

Johnson, Luke T., 'The New Testament's Anti-Jewish Slander and the Conventions of Ancient Polemic', *JBL* 108 (1989), 419-41.

Jose, Paul E., 'The Role of Gender and Gender Role Similarity in Readers' Identification with Story Characters', *Sex Roles* 21 (1989), 697-713.

Jose, Paul E., and William F. Brewer, 'Development of Story Liking: Character Identification, Suspense and Outcome Resolution', *Developmental Psychology* 20 (1984), 911-24.

Keener, Craig S., *A Commentary on the Gospel of Matthew* (Grand Rapids: Eerdmans, 1999).

Kingsbury, Jack Dean, *Matthew: Structure, Christology, Kingdom* (Philadelphia: Fortress Press, 1975).

—'The Figure of Peter in Matthew's Gospel as a Theological Problem', *JBL* 98 (1979), 67-83.

—*Jesus Christ in Matthew, Mark and Luke* (Philadelphia: Fortress Press, 1981).

—'The Figure of Jesus in Matthew's Story: A Literary-Critical Probe', *JSNT* 21 (1984), 3-36.

—'The Figure of Jesus in Matthew's Story: A Rejoinder to David Hill', *JSNT* 25 (1985), 61-85.

—'The Developing Conflict between Jesus and the Jewish Leaders in Matthew's Gospel: A Literary-Critical Study', *CBQ* 49 (1987), 57-73.

—*Matthew as Story* (Philadelphia: Fortress Press, 2nd edn, 1988).

—'On Following Jesus: The "Eager" Scribe and the "Reluctant" Disciple (Matt 2.18-22)', *NTS* 34 (1988), 45-59.

—'Reflections on "the Reader" of Matthew's Gospel', *NTS* 34 (1988), 442-60.

—'The Plot of Matthew's Story', *Int* 46 (1992), 347-56.

Levine, Amy-Jill, *The Social and Ethnic Dimensions of Matthean Salvation History: 'Go Nowhere among the Gentiles...' (Matt. 10.5b)* (Studies in the Bible and Early Christianity, 14; Lewiston, NY: Edwin Mellen Press, 1988).

Lohr, C.H., 'Oral Techniques in the Gospel of Matthew', *CBQ* 23 (1961), 403-35.

Luz, Ulrich, 'The Disciples in the Gospel According to Matthew', in Graham Stanton (ed.), *The Interpretation of Matthew* (Philadelphia: Fortress Press, 1983), 98-128.

—*Matthew 1–7: A Commentary* (trans. Wilhelm C. Linss; Minneapolis: Augsburg–Fortress, 1989).

Maher, Michael, ' "Take My Yoke upon You" (Matt. XI.29)', *NTS* 22 (1975), 97-103.

Malbon, Elizabeth Struthers, 'Fallible Followers: Women and Men in the Gospel of Mark', *Semeia* 28 (1983), 29-48.

—'Disciples/Crowds/Whoever: Markan Characters and Readers', *NovT* 28 (1986), 104-30.

—'The Jewish Leaders in the Gospel of Mark: A Literary Study of Marcan Characterization', *JBL* 108 (1989), 259-81.

McCracken, David, 'Character in the Boundary: Bakhtin's Interdividuality in Biblical Narratives', *Semeia* 63 (1993), 29-42.

—*The Scandal of the Gospels: Jesus, Story, and Offense* (New York: Oxford University Press, 1994).

Meier, John P., *The Vision of Matthew* (New York: Paulist Press, 1979).

Meeks, Wayne A., 'A Hermeneutics of Social Embodiment', *HTR* 79 (1986), 176-86.

Menninger, Richard E., *Israel and the Church in the Gospel of Matthew* (New York: Peter Lang, 1994).

Minear, Paul S., 'The Disciples and the Crowds in the Gospel of Matthew', *Anglican Theological Review*, Supplementary Series, 3 (1974), 28-44.

—*Matthew: The Teacher's Gospel* (New York: Pilgrim Press, 1982).

Moore, Stephen D., *Literary Criticism and the Gospels: The Theoretical Challenge* (New Haven: Yale University Press, 1989).

Morson, Gary Saul, and Caryl Emerson, *Mikhail Bakhtin: Creation of a Prosaics* (Stanford: Stanford University Press, 1990).

O'Day, Gail R., 'Surprised by Faith: Jesus and the Canaanite Woman', *Listening* 24 (1989), 290-301.

Orton, David E., *The Understanding Scribe: Matthew and the Apocalyptic Ideal* (JSNTSup, 25; Sheffield: JSOT Press, 1989).

Overman, J. Andrew, *Matthew's Gospel and Formative Judaism: The Social World of the Matthean Community* (Philadelphia: Fortress Press, 1990).

Patte, Daniel, *The Gospel According to Matthew: A Structural Commentary on Matthew's Faith* (Philadelphia: Fortress Press, 1987).

Powell, Mark Allan, 'Toward a Narrative-Critical Understanding of Matthew', *Int* 46 (1992), 341-46.

Pregeant, Russell, *Christology beyond Dogma: Matthew's Christ in Process Hermeneutic* (Semeia Supplements, 7; Philadelphia: Fortress Press, 1978).

Przybylski, Benno, *Righteousness in Matthew and his World of Thought* (SNTSMS, 41; Cambridge: Cambridge University Press, 1980).

Reed, Walter L., *Dialogues of the Word: The Bible as Literature According to Bakhtin* (New York: Oxford University Press, 1993).

Rhoads, David M., 'The Gospel of Matthew. The Two Ways: Hypocrisy or Righteousness', *Currents in Theology and Mission* 19 (1992), 453-61.

Sanders, E.P., *Jesus and Judaism* (Philadelphia: Fortress Press, 1985).

Shepherd, David, 'The Authority of Meanings and the Meanings of Authority: Some Problems in the Theory of Reading', *Poetics Today* 7 (1986), 129-45.

—'Bakhtin and the Reader', in Ken Hirschkop and David Shepherd (eds.), *Bakhtin and Cultural Theory* (Manchester: Manchester University Press, 1989), 91-108.

Smith, Robert Houston, 'Matthew's Message for Insiders: Charisma and Commandment in a First-Century Community', *Int* 46 (1992), 229-39.

Snodgrass, Klyne R., 'Matthew's Understanding of the Law', *Int* 46 (1992), 368-78.

Stanton, Graham N., *A Gospel for a New People: Studies in Matthew* (Edinburgh: T. & T. Clark, 1992).

—'The Communities of Matthew', *Int* 46 (1992), 379-91.

Strecker, Georg, 'The Concept of History in Matthew', in Graham Stanton (ed.), *The Interpretation of Matthew* (Philadelphia: Fortress Press, 1983), 67-84.

Syreeni, Kari, 'Between Heaven and Earth: On the Structure of Matthew's Symbolic Universe', *JSNT* 40 (1990), 3-13.

Tannehill, Robert C., 'The Disciples in Mark: The Function of a Narrative Role', *JR* 57 (1977), 386-405.

Tompkins, Jane P., 'The Reader in History: The Changing Shape of Literary Response', in Jane P. Tompkins (ed.), *Reader Response Criticism: From Formalism to Post-Structuralism* (Baltimore: The Johns Hopkins University Press, 1980), 201-32.

Van Tilborg, Sjef, *The Jewish Leaders in Matthew* (Leiden: E.J. Brill, 1972).

Via, Dan O., Jr, 'Structure, Christology, and Ethics in Matthew', in Richard A. Spencer (ed.), *Orientation by Disorientation: Studies in Literary Criticism and Biblical Literary Criticism* (Pittsburgh: Pickwick Press, 1980), 199-215.

—'Ethical Responsibility and Human Wholeness in Matthew 25.31-46', *HTR* 80 (1987), 79-100.

—*Self-Deception and Wholeness in Paul and Matthew* (Philadelphia: Fortress Press, 1990).

—*The Revelation of God and/as Human Reception in the New Testament* (Harrisburg, PA: Trinity Press International, 1997).

Vincent, John James, 'Discipleship and Synoptic Studies', *TZ* 16 (1960), 456-569.

Weaver, Dorothy Jean, *Matthew's Missionary Discourse: A Literary Critical Analysis* (JSNTSup, 38; Sheffield: JSOT Press, 1990).

Wilkins, Michael J., *The Concept of Disciple in Matthew's Gospel as Reflected in the Use of the Term* Mathētēs (Leiden: E.J. Brill, 1988).

INDEX OF AUTHORS